TWAYNE'S WORLD AUTHORS SERIES
A Survey of the World's Literature

GERMANY

Ulrich Weisstein, Indiana University
EDITOR

German Poetic Realism

TWAS 605

Front cover of second edition of Raabe's *Chronik der Sperlings-gasse*, Berlin, 1858 (*Courtesy of* Bildarchiv Preußischer Kultur-besitz, Berlin)

GERMAN
POETIC REALISM

By CLIFFORD ALBRECHT BERND

University of California, Davis

TWAYNE PUBLISHERS

A DIVISION OF G. K. HALL & CO., BOSTON

Library of Congress Cataloging in Publication Data

Bernd, Clifford A.
German poetic realism.

(Twayne's world authors series ; TWAS 605 : Germany)
Bibliography: p. 138-46
Includes index.
1. German literature—19th century—History and criticism.
2. Realism in literature.   I. Title.
PT345.B46   831'.8'0912   80- 23509
ISBN 0–8057–6447–X

for
VICTOR LANGE

Men Aaret 1848 havde en afgørende aandelig Betydning. . . . Dette Aar er den røde Skillelinje, som literært deler det 19. Aarhundrede og sætter Tidsskel.

(The year 1848 was of decisive cultural importance. . . . That year is the Rubicon which divides the literature of the 19th century. It is the demarcation of a new era.)

—Georg Brandes, writing about literary developments in Germany, in the fifth revised edition of *Hovedstrømninger i det nittende Aarhundredes Literatur* (1924).

Contents

About the Author

Clifford Albrecht Bernd was born in Bronxville, New York in 1929. He took his doctorate at the University of Heidelberg, where he studied with Paul Böckmann and Hans-Georg Gadamer. From 1958 to 1964 he taught at Princeton University. He is now professor of German at the University of California, Davis. From 1965 to 1976 he served as chairman of the Department of German and Russian. In 1977 he was a visiting fellow at the University of Leicester.

His publications include a monograph entitled *Theodor Storm's Craft of Fiction* (University of North Carolina Press, 1963; 2nd ed., 1966), a three-volume critical edition of the literary correspondence between Storm and Nobel Prize–winner Paul Heyse (Berlin, 1969–1974), and a number of articles on other German writers.

Preface

I wish to preface this study, first of all, with an expression of gratitude to the memory of Walter Silz and Edwin K. Bennett. The former I had the privilege of knowing for many years; with the latter I had the pleasure of corresponding. For decades the pioneering books of these two specialists have been standard works of reference on the subject of German Poetic Realism, and I have learned much from them. Indeed, without the constant companionship of these two volumes over a period of many years, I would never have been able to write this study. My debt to these two predecessors remains unabated even when I part company with them. Scholarship, as the noted German sociologist Max Weber once said, seeks to be surpassed. To be surpassed is not only our fate, but our universal aim; we cannot work without hoping that others will advance further than we did.[1]

The most crucial single difference between my study and those of my two predecessors relates to the treatment of the genesis of German Poetic Realism. Neither Silz nor Bennett sees the movement emerging as a result of the revolutions of 1848; they predate its inception by many years. Yet I would contend that the entire literary movement is put out of focus if its revolutionary beginning in 1848 is ignored. A good case in point is Annette von Droste-Hülshoff's prerevolutionary novella *Die Judenbuche* (The Jews' Beech-Tree). It is not, as Bennett and Silz have argued, a monument of Poetic Realism, but rather a work which should be consciously deleted from any account of the movement, for German Poetic Realism outrightly rejected the mystical, supernatural premises which give that novella its elusive form.

The time has come, I believe, to focus sharply on the Phoenix-like birth of German Poetic Realism out of the ashes of 1848, and to keep its purpose and achievement clear by excluding from it works that belong to a different context.

Next in this preface, I wish to record my indebtedness to the discussion of the theory of German nineteenth-century realism which has been so enormously active in academic circles during the

1970s. The debate had received its greatest impetus with the publication, in 1971, of the first volume of Friedrich Sengle's encyclopedic study on the *Biedermeierzeit* (the Metternichian period of restoration in German literature prior to the revolutions of 1848). Never before in literary criticism had so much attention been given to the great watershed of 1848 as has been the case in the flood of studies which have followed in the wake of Sengle's book. Suddenly it became fashionable in literary criticism to speak of the 1848 political revolutions and of Julian Schmidt's new theory of literature which had been provoked by their outbreak. A host of new studies has now appeared calling attention to the literary theory that arose out of the ashes of 1848. I have learned much from this critical debate, which has made it abundantly clear that the place of Poetic Realism in the German-speaking world can only be found after 1848. German Poetic Realism, we now know, would not be a fixed unit in literary history if it did not exemplify the theory of 1848 from which it started. There can be no return to the positions of Silz, Bennett, and others of their generation.

Indebted as I am to this new focus, it has reached, I think, a point of diminishing returns. So much attention has now been devoted to the emergence of a theory of German Poetic Realism in 1848 that the aesthetic practice of the movement is becoming obscured, as Poetic Realism is being equated with its theory, and not its art. The study of literary theory has displaced the study of literature. To read the recent publications of Ulf Eisele, Hermann Kinder, Helmuth Widhammer (see bibliography), and others is to gather the distinct impression that Poetic Realism can best be understood by examining the literary theory kindled by the fires of 1848. The immortal poetic achievements of the movement, in contrast, are left to perish by the wayside.

The supposition on which this almost exclusive preoccupation with the theory of 1848 rests is, I think, wrong; for Poetic Realism exists as much in its practice as in its theory. It is as much exoteric as it is esoteric. Indeed, if the reception accorded to Poetic Realism during the last 130 years is to count for anything, it has shown that the poetic creations of the movement are what have made the great impact upon generations of readers, and not the theory. The literary movement is to be sought, therefore, primarily in the great concourse of writers who have given it its living existence, and also in the way their works have been received. If the claim can be made that the stream of German Poetic Realism is clearest near the theoretical spring from which it gushes forth, an even better argument can be put forward to show that the movement is more equable, richer, and stronger when its bed has become deep, broad, and full with its wealth of novellas, lyrics, and novels. Hence, I think the time has come when the maturation of the theoretical seed of German Poetic Realism into a living literature should be given no less attention than the germination of the theory which brought the movement into existence.

Third, I should like to express my appreciation to the authorities of the University of Leicester, and the members of its German Department, for an appointment as visiting fellow in German in 1977. The seminars on Poetic Realism I gave at Leicester, as well as the lectures on the subject which I delivered at several other British universities during my stay in England, helped immeasurably in the shaping of this monograph. The opportunities I had to present my thoughts within strict time limits forced me to concentrate on the interpretation of the literary gems of German Poetic Realism and to pass over the movement's less spectacular writings. Similarly, I felt obliged to emphasize the writers who genuinely belong to the post-1848 movement and to exclude authors such as Jeremias Gotthelf, Franz Grillparzer, Friedrich Hebbel, Eduard Mörike, and Adalbert Stifter, who, though they produced literary works after 1848, clearly have their literary worlds in the earlier Metternichian period of restoration. I realized, too, that any argument addressed to the practice of German Poetic Realism had to dwell first on the genre of the novella. That was the movement's most representative literary form. The lyric, not as peculiar to the movement but certainly no less distinguished in Germany at the time, had to be treated secondarily. Since the number of good novels that German Poetic Realism had produced was small and, hence, far less representative of the movement, it seemed logical that the discussion of the novel should trail that of the novella and the lyric. The deplorable condition into which the drama had fallen in the middle of the nineteenth century, not only in Germany but in all Europe (except Scandinavia), made it easy to omit references to that genre.

CLIFFORD ALBRECHT BERND

University of California, Davis

Acknowledgments

Siegfried Mews, the editor of the *Studies in the Germanic Languages and Literatures* at the University of North Carolina, gave me permission to reprint and slightly alter the translation of Storm's "Meeresstrand" by J. W. Thomas. The Frederick Ungar Publishing Company in New York allowed me to reproduce D. G. Wright's translation of Keller's "Abendlied." The C. W. Daniel Company, Ltd., of London permitted me to quote the translation of Fontane's "Ausgang" by Charles Fillingham Coxwell.

My faithful student Richard Hacken struggled with my palimpsestic scripts and checked innumerable references. Susan Martin of the Leicester University Press read various drafts of my manuscript and offered many constructive suggestions. Ulrich Weisstein, the editor of the series in which this book appears, generously advised me without ever insisting, and was virtually always right.

Chronology

1848   In March the revolution breaks out in German-speaking Europe. Julian Schmidt becomes editor of the *Grenzboten* and opens his campaign to promote Poetic Realism. Withering attack on the Catholic novel of François René de Chateaubriand. Rejection of the Danish playwright Henrik Hertz.

1849   Schmidt censures the Protestant novel of Wilhelm Meinhold. Critique of Berthold Auerbach's school of literature. Condemnation of William Harrison Ainsworth's Gothic novel. Gottfried Keller lives through a reign of revolutionary terror in the university town of Heidelberg. Otto Ludwig witnesses the eruption of anarchy in Saxony. Theodor Storm rebels against the Crown of Denmark.

1850   Schmidt assails the writers of March 1848, Ferdinand Freiligrath and Alexander von Ungern-Sternberg. Danish troops crush the rebellion of the German-speaking minority in the Duchy of Schleswig. Storm publishes his novella *Immensee*.

1851   Keller publishes his *Neuere Gedichte*.

1852   Schmidt repudiates Karl Gutzkow's novel *Die Ritter vom Geiste*. Storm publishes his *Gedichte*. Klaus Groth's *Quickborn* appears. Theodor Fontane's anthology of verse *Deutsches Dichteralbum*.

1853   First edition of Georg Scherer's verse anthology *Deutscher Dichterwald*. Storm forced into political exile.

1854   Peak year for emigrants from German-speaking lands seeking to escape the poverty brought on by the revolutions. Wilhelm Raabe arrives in Berlin and observes the pall of despair hanging over the city. Expanded edition of Keller's *Neuere Gedichte*. First version of Keller's novel *Der grüne Heinrich* begins to appear.

1855–   Otto Ludwig writes the first of two critical essays on "Poetic
1856   Realism."

1856   Second, augmented edition of Storm's *Gedichte*. Hermann Masius compiles ninth edition of Echtermeyer's *Auswahl deutscher Gedichte.* Publication of Keller's first volume of novellas, *Die Leute von Seldwyla,* including the masterpiece *Romeo und Julia auf dem Dorfe.* Otto Ludwig's novel *Zwischen Himmel und Erde* appears. Raabe's novel *Die Chronik der Sperlingsgasse* published.

1858   Fourth edition of Fontane's anthology *Deutsches Dichter-album.* English critic George Henry Lewes addresses himself to the emergence of realism in contemporary German fiction.

1859   Schmidt's dismissal of Annette von Droste-Hülshoff's novella *Die Judenbuche.*

1864   Raabe defects from the movement with his moralizing novel *Der Hungerpastor.*

1865   Death of Otto Ludwig.

1869   Schmidt ridicules Paul Heyse's aesthetic idealism.

1870   Storm's *Hausbuch aus deutschen Dichtern seit Claudius.*

1872   Schmidt reinforces his assault on Heyse.

1874   Julius Rodenberg starts his journal *Deutsche Rundschau.* Second volume of *Die Leute von Seldwyla* appears.

1876   Storm's novella *Aquis submersus.*

1879–   Conrad Ferdinand Meyer's novella *Der Heilige.* Final ver-
1880   sion of Keller's novel *Der grüne Heinrich* in four volumes.

1882   Definitive collection of Meyer's verse: *Gedichte.*

1883   Keller's *Gesammelte Gedichte.* Last augmented edition of Groth's *Quickborn.*

1884   Fritz Lemmermayer compiles his anthology *Die deutsche Lyrik der Gegenwart.*

1885   Final edition of Storm's *Gedichte.*

1886   Death of Julian Schmidt.

1887   Eugen Wolff issues a set of ten guidelines for the reform of German literature.

1888   Storm dies shortly after having completed his last novella, *Der Schimmelreiter.*

1889   Fontane's poem "Ausgang."

1890   Death of Keller.

1891   Masius compiles thirtieth edition of Echtermeyer's *Auswahl deutscher Gedichte.* Publication of the last landmark of German Poetic Realism, Meyer's novella *Angela Borgia.* Meyer also publishes his last important revised (fourth) edition of

Gedichte. Fontane's social novel *Unwiederbringlich* rings down the curtain on the literary movement of 1848.

1894 Sixteenth edition of Scherer's *Deutscher Dichterwald*.

CHAPTER 1

The Genesis of German Poetic Realism

I *The Movement and the Question of Its Origin*

HISTORIANS of European literature have referred to the existence of three national forms of Poetic Realism: one in Denmark, another in Sweden, and a third in Germany. The Danish movement, beginning in the 1820s, preceded the other two chronologically, but it did not survive for more than a decade.[1] Its Swedish namesake was inspired by the critical debate in Sweden in the 1830s and gathered particular momentum with the coming of the *Signatur-poeterna* (the "pseudonym poets") in the 1860s; after that its currents petered out into timid trickles which, however, lasted until the early twentieth century.[2] German Poetic Realism emerged right after the political revolutions of 1848 and dominated the literary scene in the German-speaking world for approximately forty years.

This was a unique literary movement, differing in its course not only remarkably from its Danish and Swedish counterparts, but standing out also in stark contrast to the great literatures of England, France, and Russia after the middle of the nineteenth century. The names of Dickens and Thackeray in England, Balzac and Flaubert in France, and Dostoevsky and Tolstoy in Russia quickly reveal that the most conspicuous men of letters in those three countries at the time were novelists. In Germany things were different. German literature's excellence in the second half of the nineteenth century did not lie in the production of an impressive number of novels. Instead, the distinction of German literature at the time is to be found in the happy combination of its novellas, lyrics, and the occasional novel. Particularly with the novella of Poetic Realism, Germany had something unique to offer. No form of literature was a greater favorite with the best German authors of the time or drew

17

more attention from critics after the middle of the nineteenth century. The result was that a new strain of fiction developed which shared little but its name and a certain poetic consciousness with the masterpieces of Boccaccio and Cervantes or with those of earlier German writers such as Goethe, Kleist, and Tieck.

But if Germany succeeded in producing a strikingly unique movement in imaginative literature after the middle of the nineteenth century, this movement also enjoyed the dubious distinction of having proven difficult to understand. Even the specialists have not easily recognized the precise nature of German Poetic Realism; they have been unsure about its origin; and they have differed about which authors should be included, or excluded, in the canvas of artistic works which give it its distinct historical identity.

Walter Silz, for instance, in his classic study on *Realism and Reality*, sees this literary movement beginning as early as 1817, for he includes Clemens Brentano's *Geschichte vom braven Kasperl und dem schönen Annerl* (The Story of the Just Casper and Fair Annie), which appeared in that year, in his choice of "significant examples of Poetic Realism." He then goes on to say: "Brentano's *Kasperl und Annerl* appeared in the year of Storm's birth [1817], [Hauptmann's] *Bahnwärter Thiel* [Flagman Thiel] just seventy years later [1887]; within that span, one may say, lies the achievement of Poetic Realism."[3]

E. K. Bennett's *History of the German Novelle*, which has likewise become an almost indispensable handbook for those wishing to learn about Poetic Realism in Germany, sees the movement as budding in 1839 with Karl Immermann's *Der Oberhof* (The Oberhof) and then flowering in 1842 with Annette von Droste-Hülshoff's *Die Judenbuche* (The Jews' Beech-Tree): "If *Der Oberhof* stands half-way between Jung Deutschland and Poetic Realism, and still with some rags of undiscarded Romanticism hanging about it," Bennett claims, "Droste-Hülshoff's Novelle can be said to represent Poetic Realism in a form which is hardly surpassed by anyone except perhaps by Gottfried Keller."[4]

There can, of course, be no doubt about the fact that Brentano (1778–1842), Immermann (1796–1840), and Droste-Hülshoff (1797–1848) are figures of considerable stature in German literary history; but to assign them a significant role in German Poetic Realism, or even, for that matter, to grant them a minute function in the shaping of the movement, is to arrive at a somewhat distorted picture of that movement, which simply did not arise before the political revolutions of 1848. Since Brentano, Immermann, and Droste-Hülshoff had not only published before that time, but had actually died by then, they could not possibly be a part of the new movement. To include them in any account of German Poetic Realism is to overlook the fact that 1848 marked the end of an era, not only in politics, but in literature as well. The Danish critic Georg Brandes (1842–1927), with his ingenious sense of literary history, long ago observed, clearly and accurately, that the year 1848 was the "Rubicon" which divided German literature of the nineteenth century.[5] His comment deserves to be taken seriously. After the fires of revolution had ignited, things were no longer the same in German letters; if the forms of the past were not dead, they were certainly no longer fashionable. The authors wishing to establish themselves in this changed atmosphere had to write quite differently from those whose ideals had been choked off by the upheaval. Thus, in 1848, a new literary climate began to prevail. It was the climate which gave rise to Poetic Realism.

The confusion of the specialists about the nature of German Poetic Realism has come about, it would seem, because the genesis of the movement in 1848 has not received the careful attention it requires. Only after we have properly understood the fountainhead of German Poetic Realism can we fully comprehend which authors belong in its stream and which ones lie outside its banks; for the stream is clearest near its spring and its beginnings are the measure of its capabilities.

II *The Development of Julian Schmidt's Theory of Poetic Realism*

No one in Germany in 1848, or in the years immediately following, was more forceful in ushering in the new literary mode than was the militant Prussian critic Julian Schmidt (1818–1886). He was the architect of the movement's theory; and the allegiance to his principles, either expressed or implied, constitutes the strong cable that runs through the works of German Poetic Realism. The specialist studies addressed to Poetic Realism have been all too hesitant about giving Schmidt the recognition he deserves for launching this new vehicle of literary expression;[6] such lack of recognition of the movement's theoretical father has made it difficult to view the epoch in its proper perspective. Henry Remak has rightly pointed to Schmidt's critical prowess, and the lack of attention that has been paid to it, with regard to the reception of French realism;[7] but both Schmidt's outstanding critical performance with respect to French realism, and the curious fact that he has been underrated, have been duplicated in Germany.

A century earlier the situation was quite different, for during Schmidt's lifetime there was full awareness of the weight his pen carried. The famous Prussian author Theodor Fontane (1819–1898) categorically declared in 1878 that Schmidt was the most influential living critic and also noted that even Germany's Iron Chancellor, Bismarck, admired the effectiveness of Schmidt's writing.[8] The German Socialist leader Ferdinand Lassalle (1825–1864), though Schmidt was anathema to him personally, likened the critic to a recognized primate and an anointed king; in matters of literary history, Lassalle said, Schmidt's authority was practically undisputed and almost canonically accepted.[9] But however widely Schmidt's critical acumen was recognized and acknowledged in the preceding century, it was left principally to Wilhelm Dilthey (1833–1911) and Gustav Freytag (1816–1895) to relate his prolific and influential talent to the birth of German Poetic Realism. Dilthey, a man of uncommon ability in matters of literary judgment himself, emphatically stated that no one who had witnessed events in Germany during the middle of the nineteenth century would deny "that Schmidt had been victorious" in the struggle to change the course of German literature after 1848.[10] Freytag echoed Dilthey's claim, but did so more circumstantially—due, no doubt, to his greater familiarity with Schmidt's accomplishments. Freytag stated that the amelioration of German literature after 1848 did not come about simply as a natural consequence of the revolutions of that year, but, more importantly, because of Schmidt's dogged attacks on what was amiss in German literature and, no less, because of his concomitant literary prescriptions to remedy the situation. As a result, Freytag said, Schmidt had become a successful mentor to the younger authors who were to be the standardbearers of the new literature.[11]

Schmidt's campaign to promote Poetic Realism in Germany began at the crest of the 1848 revolutionary euphoria. On March 14, 1848, for reasons directly attributable to the hostilities, he suddenly became the editor of the *Grenzboten*, a journal for politics and literature. Only the day before, Prince Clemens von Metternich, the symbol of intransigency in Vienna for some forty years, had been toppled. Munich was in an uproar; as a result the King of Bavaria would abdicate in less than a week. In Berlin tensions were mounting by the hour; in just a few days the seemingly invincible Prussian army would evacuate the capital. Schmidt, in his first public statement as editor, wrote that it was a time in which "the most unheard-of dreams had become reality."[12] The statement was significant, for it revealed Schmidt's conviction that the current reality, in the wake of the political ferment, was all that counted.

In literature it was to count no less than in politics, as Schmidt explains in the July 1848 issue of the *Grenzboten*.[13] Prior to the revolutions, he claims, "public life had been so wretched" that the public had taken refuge in an "abstract literature"; romantic literature, with its blissful divertissements of the imagination, provided an escape from an oppressive social order. But recent events, in Schmidt's thinking, had now suddenly and drastically altered the course of *belles-lettres*; the world of politics, he believes, had at last become the domain of every literate citizen, and consequently no literature of fantasy or escape should be tolerated any longer. On the contrary, the mission of literature was now to become "engulfed in life itself."

On the subsequent pages of the *Grenzboten* Schmidt expounds his new theory of literature with unflagging zest and elaborates upon it further; but never once does he lose sight of his goal: to encourage a new literature as an antidote to the one in vogue prior to the revolutions of 1848. In the same July 1848 issue of the journal he delivered a withering attack on French literature, particularly as represented by François René de Chateaubriand (1768–1848) and his cohorts.[14] Schmidt took them to task for missing the point in their portrayal of reality. They depict reality, he says, only in order to contrast it with their belief, or, for some, with the object of their disbelief: "the Catholic conception of heaven juxtaposed in purity against the base life on earth." Since a strong religious faith—or the ostentatious rejection of one—thus becomes the central issue at stake in portraying reality, the latter is subordinated to the former; and consequently, Schmidt concludes, the French have not actually taken the real world seriously.

His most aggressive early attempt to effect a change came in autumn 1848, when he delivered a vehement attack on contem-

porary Danish literature.[15] The muse of Germany's immediate
neighbor to the north was at the time dominated by the versatile
aesthetician Johan Ludvig Heiberg (1791–1860). As ruler of the
Danish Parnassus, Heiberg presided over a literature that had suddenly acquired an affluence felt far beyond Denmark's national
boundaries. It was a literature that emphasized amusement and
sentimentality, and correspondingly deemphasized politics and phi-
losophy; it was a literature that cherished farcical exposition, the-
atrical improbabilities, and speculative pleasantries; and it was a
literature that succeeded in giving rise to a dazzling array of hilarious
musical comedies and ebulliently fantastic fairy tales that were without rival on the European literary scene.

To this literature Schmidt took exception. As the specific target
of his criticism he singled out Henrik Hertz (1798–1870), the Danish
author most closely identified with Heiberg. In early 1848 Hertz's
Svend Dyrings Hus (Svend Dyring's House), a quixotic play based
on medieval ballads, had been translated into German by Friedrich
August Leo (1820–1898), an influential relative of the poet Heinrich
Heine (1797–1856). Schmidt expressed his alarm, for he feared that
this romantic pastiche, which seemed to him to be completely out
of tune with the realism called for by the revolutions, might now
find the same widespread appeal in Germany that it had received
in Denmark. He deemed it necessary, therefore, to issue a warning
to the German public about the unrealistic nature of contemporary
Danish literature in general, and of this work in particular. *Svend
Dyrings Hus*, we are told, "lacks the bold strokes" which are essential in a work of literature. The play, as well as the whole of
modern Danish literature, is "musical," and not "plastic" as it should
be. It would have been better, Schmidt says, if Hertz had transferred his poetic view from the "nocturnal side of nature" to the
"animated world of daylight." But as the play now stands, it is so
devoid of realism that it resembles life in no way. Only those works,
he adds, which are distinguished by a felicity of realism in their
treatment are capable of conveying a genuine poetic sensation to
the reader. Picturesquely, he sums up his criticism by saying:
"There beats more poetry in the pitter-patter of a simple fisher-
maiden's heart than in the stiff grandezza of all the phantoms in
history, from the prophet Samuel right on down to the seeress of
Prevorst in the nineteenth century, not forgetting the witches of
the Middle Ages."

Less striking than Schmidt's censure of contemporary French and Danish literature, but no less illustrative of the literary reform he wished to achieve, is the mixed blessing he bestowed on Wilhelm Meinhold (1797–1851), one of the popular German authors of the day. In the first *Grenzboten* issue of 1849 Schmidt reviewed Meinhold's latest novel, *Sidonie von Bork, die Klosterhexe* (Sidonia the Sorceress), adding his own measured voice of enthusiasm to the large contemporary chorus of Meinhold eulogies.[16] Schmidt is able to point to a highly successful depiction of historical reality in the work, even down to minute detail. But this praise, as he impresses upon the reader, must also be tempered with the sobering realization that Meinhold's conception of reality is not always genuine. At times it degenerates into a feigned reality that clearly feeds on the sermonizing purposes of a Protestant clergyman turned poet. Schmidt intends thus to warn us that Meinhold's poetic reality could delude us into believing, at first sight, that the real world had been portrayed; but further insight would show, Schmidt says, that the author was more interested in a supernatural world than in the observable one.

The summer of 1849 brought another significant step in the furtherance of Schmidt's theory of Poetic Realism. It came in the form of a critique of Berthold Auerbach (1812–1882) and the latter's fashionable "school" of literature.[17] This essay sets itself against the "poets of detail," as the school's adherents are called. Since the previous summer, immediately following the revolutions, Schmidt had felt compelled to criticize publicly Auerbach's collection of *Schwarzwälder Dorfgeschichten* (Village Tales from the Black Forest), the first volume of which had appeared in 1843, and the second in early 1848. Because these prerevolutionary tales were attracting European attention, Schmidt wished to make the public aware that they did not convey a universally accepted picture of reality: they are only offbeat images of provincial import, for the minutiae of rural Black Forest life, however lovingly portrayed by Auerbach, represent no more than a small corner of the world. Auerbach may have succeeded in capturing a few picturesque moments of real life, but his reality holds up solely under the guise of local color, and it breaks down abruptly on being transported to the broad, actual life of the general public.

Schmidt reiterates this position, when, in the same essay, he objects to Leopold Kompert's prerevolutionary collection of tales entitled *Aus dem Ghetto* (Tales from the Ghetto), which had also been published in 1848. Schmidt considers Kompert (1822–1886) to be one of Auerbach's most gifted imitators: like Auerbach, he focuses on the authenticity and the ethnic character of a local region, or on the mundane realities of life in a far corner of Germany. Schmidt admits that Kompert paints the life and manners of his native Jewish settlement in German-speaking Bohemia with warmth and accuracy. Yet these charming descriptions and delightful anecdotes are so rigidly limited to the "stagnating, narrow pond of the ghetto" that they, too, remain far removed from the fresh, broad "mainstream of life." They represent, therefore, unique and idealized situations of reality rather than reality itself.

Schmidt's position in defining his theory of Poetic Realism with regard to the realism of Auerbach and Kompert may thus be summed up as follows: although Auerbach in the *Schwarzwälder Dorfgeschichten* and Kompert in *Aus dem Ghetto* have depicted daily life in a seemingly authentic manner, they have nevertheless done so imperfectly, for their truth, restricted to the idyllic world of the peasants in the Black Forest or to the inhabitants of isolated Jewish communities in Bohemia, constitutes only a partial picture of reality, separated from the "mainstream of life"; consequently it is mixed with falsehood. Finally, if Auerbach's and Kompert's fictional achievements are not completely "real," they also are not completely "poetic."[18]

The climax in Schmidt's stubborn insistence that literature, if it is to be poetic, must also be realistic came a few months later when he turned to English literature and condemned William Harrison Ainsworth's Gothic novel *The Lancashire Witches*. The reception accorded to this English novel by its German readers had been spectacular. Almost simultaneously with its publication in England in 1849, an English-language edition was printed in Leipzig; and virtually at once three different publishing houses commissioned translations into German. The enthusiastic reception in Germany of this novel, which reveled in feats of incredible supernaturalism, must have horrified Schmidt, for with great haste he set out to countervail Ainsworth's sudden popularity by circulating a review in which he dismissed the novel most contemptuously.[19] Ainsworth (1805–1882) is "unsurpassed," he says, when it comes to "conjuring up the horrors of hell." Drawing on *The Lancashire Witches* and five other works by Ainsworth, Schmidt shows how unsparingly the

English novelist presses upon his reader a dazzling phantasmagoria of witches, devils, ghosts, exotic spirits, spurious romances, phantastic prophecies, spells, and curses; in short, the very antithesis of what is real. Yet of all of Ainsworth's literary capers, in Schmidt's estimation, the ultimate romantic *embarras de richesse* occurs in *The Lancashire Witches*. To Schmidt, this novel is sheer madness; far too long, he goes on to say, has such "insanity in fictional form" been tolerated by the German reading public. "The nightmare of madness," he concludes, "belongs in the lunatic asylum"; it should not find a haven "in the sunlight of fiction."

By 1850, with this frenzied denunciation of Ainsworth's novel, Schmidt had become obsessively dedicated to the task of making German fiction consonant with reality as it can be universally recognized. Indeed, it may be said that in the two years since the great watershed of March 1848 he had become a messianic advocate for realistic literature.

The year 1850, however, also saw the vigorous emergence of another dimension to his campaign to promote Poetic Realism. Literature, he now argued, must not only be realistic in order to be poetic, it must also be poetic in order to be realistic. On the very first pages of the 1850 issue of the *Grenzboten* he makes this clear.[20] He addresses himself to the writers of March 1848, those *Märzpoeten* whom the revolutions had already infected and who could thus no longer content themselves with the romantic tones of prerevolutionary literature. Rejecting the conventions of pure fancy, the March writers directed their attention rather to the topical issues of the day, such as civil freedom and even revolution itself. These writers, Schmidt allows, rightly substituted reality for idealism, but at the same time they joined hands with the politicians, and in so doing lost sight of the true calling of literature. Schmidt argues that literature must not prejudice itself in favor of a single political viewpoint and thus be reduced to a cog in the partisan wheel. If the pre-March writers sought to escape from reality by conjuring up imaginative dream worlds, he says, the March writers, in revolting from the past, contented themselves all too easily with merely disclaiming the unreal attitude of prerevolutionary fiction. But it is not enough for postrevolutionary fiction to reject unrealities; the new spirit also demands a new form which is capable of enduring on a more universal scale than do patriotic sketches of provincial reality or tendentious mosaics of philosophic reflection.

Schmidt's impatience with the March writers is illustrated, in particular, by his rejection of two authors of the time, who, he felt, had fixed their gazes—and thus their literary themes—too closely upon the politico-journalistic world about them: Alexander von Ungern-Sternberg (1806–1868) and Ferdinand Freiligrath (1810–1876). The two men were actually in opposition during the strife of 1848, for Ungern-Sternberg supported the royalist camp and Freiligrath the republican faction; but both, in spite of their radical differences, committed, in Schmidt's opinion, the cardinal sin of turning the office of literature into a forum to support a specific political conviction. In reviewing Ungern-Sternberg's novel *Die Royalisten* (The Royalists), Schmidt even goes so far as to deny it the right to be called a novel.[21] According to Schmidt, this work describes the insurrection in Berlin on March 18 and 19, 1848, from a negative, royalist point of view, which, he adds, is nothing more than objectionable party politics in literary disguise.

Schmidt levels a similar criticism at Freiligrath's *Neuere sociale und politische Gedichte* (Modern Social and Political Poems), the first of which appeared in 1849. Reviewing these poems, Schmidt claims that Freiligrath has simply wasted his poetic talent.[22] All he does in these lyrics is to sprinkle "spices on the food of the democratically incited masses," which is essentially not different from what Ungern-Sternberg did for the monarchists. Of course, as Schmidt lets us know, one pugnacious turn deserves another. If royalist authors like Ungern-Sternberg try to outdo one another in heaping insults upon the heads of the republicans, then we should not be surprised to find writers of republican persuasion like Freiligrath eagerly deriding their royalist adversaries in a *quid pro quo*. But this just goes to show, Schmidt continues, that Freiligrath does not rise above the political issues of the day either, for the reality he portrays is crudely confined to a sociopolitical reality; his poetry has lapsed into propagandistic doggerel and is, therefore, "devoid of genuine artistic vitality."

With the rejection of the writers of March 1848, Schmidt's theory of Poetic Realism had attained full maturity. Now his stubborn edict that the themes and images of real life must prevail in poetic literature had been complemented by the equally harsh delineation of poetic bounds within which that reality should be depicted. On the one hand, literary excesses of fancy and escapism were condemned; on the other, realistic literature was to be shunned if its poetic substance had withered to a state of artificial incrustation. By the beginning of the 1850s, then, the ever-widening circle of *Grenzboten* readers was fully aware of what the contentious Prussian critic expected from postrevolutionary literature in Germany. Yet this does not mean that his fight to advance Poetic Realism had ended; his doctrinaire proselytizing activities continued undiminished on behalf of the new literature. As the Viennese critic Emil Kuh (1828–1876) picturesquely put it, Schmidt spurred "the horses of realism" ever onward.[23]

However, Schmidt had essentially nothing new to add to his theory after this time; all subsequent criticism is dedicated solely to the belligerent maintenance of the position he already tenaciously held. Even the best of his later reviews, his merciless condemnation of *Die Ritter vom Geiste* (The Knights of the Spirit), a novel by Karl Gutzkow (1811–1878), in 1852[24] and his brusque dismissal of Annette von Droste-Hülshoff's novella *Die Judenbuche* in 1859,[25] have, in spite of some compelling insights, nothing new to offer. Schmidt merely reminds us in these essays that reality does not preside over the execution of the details in these two works. The portrayal of Prince Egon von Hohenberg is cited as being typical of Gutzkow's runaway imagination. Schmidt finds it incredible that a character who is supposed to be a key representative of the nobility can be depicted as sitting down at a table in his castle together with a number of journeymen carpenters, jesting with them in carefree intimacy, while, at the same time, the servants of the prince's household, all in gala dress, are stiffly standing in back of the same table holding bottles of champagne in their hands. Yet scenes as unbelievable as this one, Schmidt says, occur again and again throughout Gutzkow's novel.

In Droste-Hülshoff's novella, he informs us, "the reader is left in the dark with regard to no less than four different murders; it remains unclear who committed them and why they were committed." Hence, the composition as a whole is veiled in an obscurity typical of Droste-Hülshoff's penchant for letting everything "terminate in death and for covering all the details with the dust of the grave." "That may have something to do with romanticism," he adds, "but for the reader wishing to be convinced realistically such nebulosity is too much to accept." Schmidt concludes his remarks on Droste-Hülshoff by saying that she "has misused" her talent for writing realistically.[26]

This commentary on *Die Judenbuche* is shattering for the literary historian who has been accustomed to view the work as a document of Poetic Realism rather than as an opus by a prerevolutionary "strict Catholic writer" (as Schmidt called her[27]), for whom a divinely inspired, mystical order uniting everything on earth—and all above and below it—transcended the interest she had in the more limited world of visible reality. The theory underlying this criticism, however, does not go beyond what Schmidt had developed a decade earlier. Between March 1848 and the early 1850s the leaven for the new movement in German literature had been fully prepared.

CHAPTER 2

The Novella

I *Theodor Storm*

I F it can be claimed that Julian Schmidt was the missionary apostle
of German Poetic Realism, that the impress of his hand constituted the shaping force which brought its theory into being, then
it must also be recognized that the first important practitioner of
the new literary movement was Theodor Storm (1817–1888).[1]

Storm was a native of the Danish duchy of Schleswig, and as a
consequence of this geographic stroke of fate, the conflagration of
1848 affected him more adversely than it did any other Poetic Realist
who acquired enduring fame. It could be said, in fact, that Storm
received from the revolutions his baptism by fire as a poet. This
has been more clearly seen by a Danish historian, Knud Fabricius
(1875–1967), than by the literary critics, perhaps because Fabricius
commanded a deeper insight into the Danish political and military
events of 1848–1850 which affected the course of Storm's life so
markedly.[2]

On March 24, 1848, only a few days after the revolutions had
stirred the emotions in Vienna, Munich, and Berlin, the German
inhabitants of Storm's native duchy openly revolted against their
Danish sovereign. It was, in the words of Disraeli, in a moving
speech before the House of Commons, "rebellion in the most un-
blushing and flagrant manner,"[3] and the bloodiest of all the German
insurrections to date. Julian Schmidt informed his readers that the
revolutionary movement in Germany first really came to life when
this rebellion broke out.[4] By April 20, 1848, Storm's native Husum
was occupied by Danish royalist troops seeking to crush the insurgents. The town was soon on the brink of anarchy; and for over two
years it tottered between the exigencies of mutinous warfare and
the tyranny of martial law until, finally, the bloody royalist victory

29

at Friedrichstadt, a few miles south of Husum, quelled the insurrection.

The tumult caused by this revolutionary war left its mark on Storm. He wrote vivid accounts of his anguishing experiences for a rebel newspaper.[5] As the war progressed, he became increasingly impassioned. On May 1, 1849, he demanded outright sedition against the Crown of Denmark; on October 5 of the same year he publicly refused to obey the laws handed down by the new military government.[6] Above all, the revolution, the harsh military occupation, and the oppressive political conditions which had suddenly engulfed him, all forcibly alienated him from the fairy-tale literary activity in which he had been engaged in his prerevolutionary days, while still a loyal subject of the Danish Crown.

Formerly, as a citizen of the Danish monarchy, Storm had been infected by the unrestrained fantasy which constituted such an integral part of literature in Denmark. He had not been altogether different from his illustrious contemporary, Hans Christian Andersen (1805–1875). But Danish literature, as Julian Schmidt had said, was out of tune with the rugged realities of the revolutionary times: it was a literature more "musical" than "plastic," more a part of the "nocturnal side of nature" than of the "animated world of daylight."[7]

Storm felt obliged to revolt against Danish literature as much as he revolted against the Danish Crown. Because of his impassioned experiences in the rebellion, he could no longer owe allegiance to the Crown; but neither could he continue to view literature as a flight from reality into a fairy-tale land of fantasy. Instead, the political revolution that had so adversely touched him compelled him to look for a more realistic, down-to-earth vehicle of literary expression. For this vehicle he turned his gaze away from Copenhagen and the North and directed his attention southward to Germany. There a realistic literature had suddenly sprung into being in 1848. It was the so-called *Märzliteratur*, which Schmidt saw represented by Freiligrath and Ungern-Sternberg, and which had nothing to do with a fiction of pure fantasy, but in which the topical issues of the day prevailed. Storm hurried to embrace this new realistic literature of revolutionary Germany and began to substitute the new German, down-to-earth mode of writing political poetry—he wrote, e.g., a number of important political poems—for his earlier, very Danish, literary activity of collecting and writing fairy tales, and of composing lilting rhyme and sound melodies.

But thirty years of citizenship in the Danish monarchy and an intimate familiarity with Danish poetry and prose had left an indelible mark on him (all his life he continued to read Danish literature and Danish journals). It was not at all easy for him to adapt himself to this new, political conception of literature. On the one hand, because of the political and military turmoil in which he was enmeshed, he was provoked to revolt against romantic Danish literature and to embrace the new realistic literature of Germany; on the other hand, however, because of his roots in the Danish tradition, he could not succumb for long to the temptation of turning the office of literature into a forum to voice political convictions, in the way Freiligrath and Ungern-Sternberg did in contemporary Germany.

This predicament left Storm with no alternative but to seek other forms of literature which would be more enduring than Freiligrath's or Ungern-Sternberg's outcries of momentary political anguish, and also more able to come to grips with the entrapping reality of the present than seemed possible in the sentimental literary climate that prevailed in Denmark.

The literary form to which Storm turned particularly energetically, and the one which gave him his most spectacular success, was the novella. He infused this genre, though, with notions which bear the unmistakable imprint of the moderator of Danish literature at the time, the ingenious Johan Ludvig Heiberg; and, as a consequence, Storm put the novella to a use different from that prevalent in the German tradition. Scattered throughout Heiberg's literary criticism, as Heiberg's biographer Henning Fenger points out,[8] had been statements calling for a new form of Danish prose fiction, the novella, which was to be particularly close to the drama, but which, unlike the drama or the popular fairy tale, would be neither amusing in its manner of presentation nor remote from everyday life; rather, it was to lead into the midst of genuine burgher life and deal with contemporary individuals and their problems.[9] Storm unquestionably benefited from Heiberg's prescriptions for a new, unromantic form of Danish prose having a deep inner kinship with the drama; and when he applied them, under the impact of the revolution, to the German literary scene, he became the first Poetic Realist in the German-speaking world to acquire fame quickly.

The Hungarian critic György Lukács (1885–1971) was the first to recognize that Storm had refashioned the traditional German nov-

ella. In Storm's belief, Lukács said, the German novella was no
longer what it formerly had been: the brief recounting of an event
which is made gripping by its unusual nature and has a surprising
climax.[10] Instead, the German novella was now to assume the instructive office formerly held by the drama, for the public was
increasingly a reading public which took its instruction less and less
from the secular pulpit of the stage. Like the drama, the novella
was now to have the capability of expressing the most profound
problems of human life and was to organize itself around a central
conflict common to the whole; as a consequence it would demand
the most succinct form and the exclusion of everything nonessential.
Storm's new conception of the German novella turned it into the
poetic pulpit of the moment; for in it he could poetically converse
with the public and, within the smallest imaginable compass, focus
attention upon the most essential characteristics of human destiny.
In other words, by employing the genre of the novella in this new
way, he could present to the large reading public of his time an
exceedingly sharp picture of the contours underlying external
reality.

The new theory was first successfully put into practice when he
wrote, during the revolutionary crisis of 1849, a novella entitled
Immensee. He sent the manuscript to Berlin, where an adventurous
publisher printed it in the autumn of 1850; the Prussian author and
critic Fontane commented shortly afterwards that it was one of the
greatest masterpieces of fiction he had ever read.[11] Seventy-nine
additional printings of *Immensee*, not including reprints in editions
of Storm's collected works or the many translations, followed the
speculative publication of 1850 until, finally, the copyright expired
in 1918 and it entered the public domain. Today, the novella also
lives on in Thomas Mann's immortal *Tonio Kröger*, for, as Mann
himself more than once insisted, that story is, in the last analysis,
"but a modern version of *Immensee*."[12]

A compelling reality is portrayed in Storm's novella. It is a reality
facing all mankind and from which there is no escape: the evanescence of human life and happiness. Hence, the novella offers a
poignant poetic lesson on the nature of reality; but it also steers the
reader unrelentingly into reality, for it unflinchingly marks the limits of man's abilities in coping with transience as an obtrusive force
of destruction.

With but a few bold strokes, Storm paints in this novella a picture of childhood happiness and its gradual and steady destruction by the passing of time. As long as the characters Elisabeth and Reinhard are young and in school together, they are happy. The flux of time, however, compels them to separate. As Reinhard matures in the course of the years, he leaves the primary school, where he has been together with Elisabeth, and enters a boys' secondary school. He may now only share his afterschool leisure hours with the companion of his childhood. Seven years later he is deprived even of the leisure hours, for his secondary education is completed and he moves away to study at a distant university. The reader becomes witness to Elisabeth and Reinhard's last happy day together. By the time the six ensuing months between June and December have drifted by, the previous warmth of affection between the youthful couple has faded into the forced chill of prolonged separation. The further passage of time only intensifies their estrangement; two more years sever their ties so thoroughly that Elisabeth agrees to marry someone else. The subsequent years bring Elisabeth and Reinhard to the final realization that the enchantment of their youth has gone forever.

Thus, the reader of *Immensee* is told of how human happiness erodes with the passing of time. But the novella also contains another message. Fused with this portrayal of the fragility of human happiness is a countervailing level of thought. The narrator seems to be reassured that, in spite of his sensitivity to the destructive effects of passing time, his apprehension can be overcome by the power of memory. This notion is conveyed when, on the pages that immediately precede and follow the story of the passing of human happiness, the narrator relates how Reinhard, as an old man, relives in his memory the same joyful scenes that he had once known. Through recollection the aged Reinhard can detach himself from his immediate surroundings and recapture his lost happiness as if it had not been obliterated by the action of time.

A third thought follows: closely interwoven with the portrayal of the narrator's sensitivity to the ravaging effects of passing time, and his apparent ability to ease this haunting concern through the counterweight of memory, is his awareness that this power of memory will prove deceptive. In the closing chapter of *Immensee* the reader is informed that, just as earlier happiness had eroded with the passing of time, the power of memory, too, will become engulfed in the stream of time: the aged Reinhard's memory dwells in a body

increasingly falling prey to senility and the subsequent dissolution
of death.

Here the novella ends. The poetic insight into reality which the
reader gains from *Immensee* is disquieting indeed, but there can
be no doubt that real life is acutely presented. And it is not surprising
that man's helplessness should emerge so distinctly in this realistic
portrayal, since we know that Storm composed *Immensee* in the
deep state of despair caused by the disruptive political and military
events surrounding him.

Hardly had Storm completed *Immensee*, however, when he became even more adversely affected by the mutinous turmoil. On
August 1, 1850, before *Immensee* could even be published, another
brigade of Danish royalist troops entered Husum and immediately
began to stamp out all remaining vestiges of the local insurrection.
This provoked further rebellion and more bloodshed all around the
adjacent countryside. Storm became a witness to horrible sights:
as he wrote in an anguished letter to a friend on October 14, 1850,
the wounded poured into the town, hundreds and hundreds of
them, not only soldiers but women, children, and old people, whose
bodies had been mangled, mutilated, and seared by bullets.[13] The
author grew increasingly depressed, as his letters show. He found
intolerable the new state of siege declared by the military government, and eventually felt he had no choice but to go into exile, a
fate he endured for eleven despondent years. Exile, however, only
sharpened his defeatist outlook on life, and it made him work all
the more, with unabated vigor, toward contouring the same hard
reality which had poetically shaped *Immensee*. This novella, then,
became the paradigmatic pattern for Storm's many later novellas.
The perfectly typical example of his Poetic Realism, though, is *Aquis
submersus*. Storm himself considered that novella, composed a little
over a quarter of a century after *Immensee*, to be his crowning
achievement.[14] In more recent times, none other than Hermann
Hesse felt this way, too. Recalling, only very shortly before his
death in 1962, those works of Storm which had made the most
lasting impressions on him, Hesse stated that the first one which
came to his mind was *Aquis submersus*.[15]

In *Aquis submersus*, as in its precursor, *Immensee*, the delights
of childhood are swept away by the obliterating action of time. The
joy which the main character, Johannes, had thought to be per-

manent comes to an end when the time comes for him to study abroad. In the next five years, conditions change to such an extent that the pleasures of former days prove to be gone forever. The drift of time forces the carefree happiness of youth to develop into a love encircled with fright. Johannes and the girl he loves, Katharina, hope that time will remain at a standstill; but this is precisely what it cannot do. The hours Johannes spends with Katharina in order to paint her portrait slip away with each stroke of his brush. The events which then follow rapidly one after another make it imperative for him, if he is to regain his lost bliss, to establish a home for Katharina quickly. But the more he endeavors to race against time, the more he is defeated by it. Although he is badly wounded and in need of rest, he leaves his sickbed earlier than he should in order to earn enough money to return to Katharina before Christmas. As a consequence, his wound heals so poorly that by Christmas his condition is worse. Day after day passes, as he notes with anguish, and his separation from Katharina is prolonged even further. By spring, when he is able to return, the last friend who could have helped him has died and, in a situation altogether reminiscent of *Immensee,* Katharina has married someone else. He has returned too late. In the next five years things worsen further: his illegitimate child is born, and as the ensuing days and months pass, the yearning to regain what he has lost increases. But the change of conditions brought on by the current of time thwarts this yearning, too. In the end, Johannes is compelled to realize that his dead child, the symbol of his entire life's joy, has been drowned in the inundating floods of oblivion. "Aquis submersus, aquis submersus" are the chilling words of the chorus at the end.

Complete as this engulfing process seems to be, its effects are, nevertheless, reversed when we sense its being coupled, in the poetic composition of the novella, with the countervailing force of reminiscence. The whole of the story about Johannes is preserved in a hand-written memoir that possesses the power to salvage for posterity Johannes's former happiness, long after it has been submerged in its aqueous grave of time. The reversal, however, is only temporary, for the memoir's pages yellow and fade. Symbolically, too, a motto pointing to the transitoriness of all things is inserted over the door of the house where the memoir is kept. The implication of its meaning becomes all the more trenchantly clear when

we are informed that the tongue in which it is written is an anti-
quated dialect that has ceased to be a vehicle of communication.

But just when the readers begin to realize that the memoir, too,
will fall prey to the destructive force of time, they are made to feel
that the narrator is striving to allay this fear by resorting to a further
act of memory. This time he has recourse to the most vivid means
of recalling the past that is known to him: pictorial commemoration.
Portraits record and perpetuate the identical story of Johannes's
childhood joy that seemed to be retained in the memoir. Again,
however, even though the narrator makes us realize that he can
counteract his fear of the memoir's fading by resorting to painting
as a perpetuating factor, he also lets us see that even this, his most
vivid means of salvaging Johannes's former happiness, fails to en-
dure. Worms start to eat away at the paintings' frames. Then the
paintings themselves fall apart and are thrown away. "Aquis submersus, aquis submersus" at the end applies not only to the oblit-
eration of Johannes's youthful joy and his entire life's happiness,
but to the perpetuating medium of pictorial commemoration as well.

On this disquieting note the novella ends. As with *Immensee*, the
reader of *Aquis submersus* closes the book after having been chilled
by the realistic depiction of man's ineffectual struggle against the
continuing processes of human mortality and material decay. But
the chilling is more intense, for this novella is more artfully wrought
than was its precursor. The more complex use of the filter of memory
in *Aquis submersus* constitutes the great difference between the
two novellas; it has galvanized the tension between the annihilating
and the perpetuating factors. Thus, the reading of *Aquis submersus*
constitutes a more poignant poetic experience and confronts us with
a far more engaging vision of the reality of perpetual human extinction in death.

As *Immensee* and *Aquis submersus* show, Storm was both a pioneer and an eloquent practitioner of German Poetic Realism. He
had access to a gift of poetic expression that pervaded his realism
with a thoroughly chilling sentiment. Skillfully, he combined in his
novellas the conception of authentic realism with the poetic power
of stirring drama; and, by doing so, he also refashioned the traditional German novella. On account of his achievement he became—
as Robert Zimmermann (1824–1898), the influential Austrian aesthetician of the nineteenth century, once remarked in an English
journal—the "Nestor" of German novella-writers in his time.[16]

II *Gottfried Keller*

Following quickly in the wake of Theodor Storm came Gottfried Keller (1819–1890), a Swiss writer two years Storm's junior. Keller, too, was destined to get his baptism by fire as a poet during the revolutions of 1848–1849. He had, in fact, felt the impact of revolutionary turmoil as early as November 1847, when Switzerland became embroiled in a civil war between those cantons espousing the cause of states' rights and those advocating federal supremacy. The ashes of this war had hardly cooled when, in February 1848, another insurgence broke out in Switzerland: the inhabitants of the canton of Neuchâtel rebelled against the Crown of Prussia, to which they owed allegiance, and sought to overthrow its governors within their land. All Switzerland sided with the insurrectionists, of course, in their fight against the yoke of foreign domination.

But however agitated the passions were by these revolutionary events, however much the Swiss temper was enflamed, the conflagrations were dwarfed by the insurrections which swept Paris, Vienna, and Berlin in early 1848. Keller was so electrified by these latest events of such colossal magnitude—as he called them—that he hurried to the public library in Zurich each day to absorb there with growing trepidation the assorted journalistic disquisitions concerning the spreading fires of revolt. By the beginning of October 1848, he began to wonder whether the stormy times would not gnaw at his very existence and, indeed, even uproot him.[17]

Such were his feelings when he decided to leave Switzerland to study at the University of Heidelberg, located in the Grand Duchy of Baden. It was a momentous decision, for only a few months earlier Baden had been convulsed by a terrible civil war as well, and the smoldering embers of rebellion were still everywhere to be seen. "Nothing," an eyewitness of September 1848 tells us,

can be more uneasy and disquieting than the appearance of the Duchy of Baden. In Heidelberg, ultra-revolutionary students have come to a total schism with their moderately and vaguely revolutionary professors; and it is at present difficult to see how any understanding is to be effected between teacher and scholar, so as to render the university a seat of learning of any other kind than that of subversive principles. In this part of Germany the revolutionary fermentation appears far more active, and is far more visible . . . than even in those hotbeds of revolutionary movement, Austria and Prussia.[18]

The worst, however, came after Keller entered the unhappy duchy. The ferment and agitation of 1848 continued to mount in the following year and exploded anew, more violently than before. In May 1849, the Grand Duke of Baden was forced to flee. Anarchy quickly followed, and soon the entire duchy was permeated with the vapor of cannon and the reek of blood. Heidelberg, where Keller had taken up residence, became the eerie citadel of a harsh Polish military dictator; swarms of soldiers and horses crowded into the little university town, requisitioning all available space and often sleeping in the streets. Keller now had to live through the reign of terror which befell Heidelberg's citizenry.

One of Keller's teachers at the university, Ludwig Häusser (1818–1867), vividly recorded the details.[19] The horror began in late May 1849, when guerrilla warfare erupted just north of the town. Häusser's chronicle relates that a bloodbath ensued in the entire adjacent countryside. On June 5, in neighboring Weinheim, a number of university students who had joined the rebel cause were shot down, while others committed suicide in order to avoid capture. On June 13 a ghastly slaughter occurred at nearby Waldmichelbach. Hundreds more were killed in fighting along the Neckar River near Heidelberg on June 15. As a result of the Battle of Waghäusel on June 21, innumerable men lay dead or dying on the roadsides just to the south of the town. Streams of panic-stricken civilians and soldiers, hungry, ravaged, and blackened by gunpowder, kept pouring into Heidelberg; the university hospital was filled to overflowing with the wounded.

Two days later Heidelberg itself was besieged. Keller writes of the horror which gripped the populace, and writes of the cannon which were set up right in front of his own window in an attempt to ward off the enemy attack. He describes how he witnessed the gunning down of a soldier just in front of him, and he tells how the rebel forces put the gun to their own wounded, rather than let them fall into the hands of the conquering troops.[20]

These appalling sights, which had continually manifested themselves in the chain of insurrections about Keller ever since November 1847, and which he had been forced to observe in their most gruesome form while at Heidelberg, affected him profoundly. He had been roughly initiated into the cruel realities of the day, and this could not but radically alter the course of his literary career. On July 23, 1849—the very same day that the bloody revolution in

Baden was finally and mercilessly crushed south of Heidelberg at Rastatt—Keller commented in a letter that he had made up his mind to abandon the writing of lyric poetry, for he no longer had any use for vehicles of subjective expression. Instead, he felt a longing for a form of literature oriented more toward the actuality of life, such as that he had recently witnessed; he hoped to find it in the drama.[21]

Immediately he set out to write a historical drama, *Der Sonderbund* (The Separate Alliance), which addressed itself to the first of the revolutions he had experienced. But try as he might, he did not succeed in developing the specific literary features he sought. If the lyric mode seemed to him too poetic to be in tune with the realities of the day, his attempts at writing drama seemed to be too full of local color, too devoid of the timeless poetic quality he had once found in the lyric.[22] As a consequence of his dissatisfaction with both the subjective lyric and the objective drama, Keller directed his attention increasingly to another literary form, the novella. With this new "sister of the drama," as Storm had called the novella,[23] Keller found the literary genre he was seeking.

Of all the novellas that were to bring Keller fame, none has attracted more attention than *Romeo und Julia auf dem Dorfe* (A Village Romeo and Juliet).[24] In the year of its publication, 1856, the writer Berthold Auerbach said it was "a work of art which had few equals in German literature."[25] Julian Schmidt and Theodor Storm had the same impression. Each of them called it "a gem of literature."[26] Indeed, it is an extraordinary document of Poetic Realism. It is both rich in realistic detail and unflinching in candor. If Storm's novellas addressed themselves to the problem of reality by exhibiting an astonishing willingness to grapple with the perpetual reality of death in man's life, Keller's art derives from a more tantalizing concern with the elusive nature of reality. As in Storm's tales, everything in this novella, too, is built up from a most faithful observation of actual life, but reality appears now as a contradictory mystery, in which the difficulty of distinguishing between the actual and the imaginative (always colliding with one another) is ever before the reader.

Keller had mulled over this story throughout his period of awakening to life's bitter truths while at Heidelberg. In January 1849, only a few months after his arrival, he was already busy molding it into the form of an epic poem.[27] However, following the collapse

of the Badensian revolution in July 1849, and in line with his decision
to abandon the lyric in favor of the drama, he soon aborted his plans
for making a poem out of the story and started to think of it, instead,
in terms of a dramatic idea. His impetus for the dramatic idea came
from a book by a local professor that was generating tremendous
academic excitement in Heidelberg at the time: G. G. Gervinus's
Shakespeare (1849–1850).

Gervinus (1805–1871) had proposed that the dramatic substance
of Shakespeare's *Romeo and Juliet* was derived from the collision
of the leading characters' idyllic love with the reality of the world
around them. This theory of counteraction between the subjective
realm of fancy and palpably real circumstances is postulated at the
very beginning of Gervinus's analysis of the play; for him it constitutes the dramatic linkage of all the play's disconnected scenes
as well as its many characters.[28] Gervinus's theory, however dis-
puted it turned out to be among scholars of Shakespeare, provided
Keller with the rich dramatic kernel he needed. He embraced it
at once, for this collision of chimeric reverie with the unsettling
facts of the real world expressed precisely what he himself, as a
would-be epic poet, must have agonizingly felt when he discovered
his world of complacent fantasy to be thoroughly at odds with the
reality of the revolution thundering just outside his window in Heidelberg.

Gervinus's essentially dramatic kernel did not, though, germinate
under Keller's nurture into another intricate drama. Instead, Keller
transplanted his newfound dramatic seed into the soil of the novella,
where it had good opportunity to grow. The more succinct form of
the new "sister of the drama" was able to accommodate the same
central conflict that Gervinus had seen as the source of dramatic
substance in Shakespeare's *Romeo and Juliet;* but, in addition, the
novella could be far more closely focused on the conflict itself than
could a drama, which—in Gervinus's conception—called for a
greater wealth of vivid characters, the portrayal of more variegated
scenes, and the inclusion of an array of subordinate plots. Had
Keller been as interested as Gervinus in the organic development
of the conflict between the idyllic world and external reality, he
might have written another drama. It was not the development of
this conflict, however, but the very conflict itself that Keller wished
to present; and for this purpose the novella was more suitable. In
the novella the essential conflict that Gervinus had extracted from

Shakespeare's *Romeo and Juliet* could stand out sharply, rapidly taking on bold relief devoid of everything nonessential.

Keller critics have been surprisingly reticent about noting the importance of Gervinus's theory for the inception of *Romeo und Julia auf dem Dorfe*. In spite of Keller's comment that he had found in Gervinus's book a rich lode of ideas for further embellishment—precisely at the time when the composition of this novella was shaping up in his mind[29]—the critics have preferred to point to an account in a Zurich newspaper of 1847 as the narrative's sole source. This traditional thesis is in need of emendation, for while it is true that the colorless newspaper account did have a bearing on the epic poem Keller wanted to write prior to his harrowing experience in the midst of civil war, the actual seed out of which the stirring novella grew—indeed which even supplied its title—sprang rather from Gervinus's exciting commentary on Shakespeare's *Romeo and Juliet*. While Gervinus's theory corresponded to what Keller had experienced during the Badensian revolution, the newspaper article did not. Keller's own revolution in prose—by which the pithy, dramatic form of the novella was to supplant the long drawn-out verse narrative—demanded that a crisp dramatic conflict, such as the one postulated by Gervinus, should replace the pallid newspaper report as the poetic center around which the new composition could uniformly revolve.

The novella is divided into two parts which are wholly irreconcilable: the first dominated by two farmers' selfish real-estate interests, and the second—so discordantly different—by two young adolescents' fairy-tale-like love for one another. The initial realistic description of simple peasants, centered around their greed and cutthroat competition for land possession, is superseded by their children's pursuit of a quixotic dream of love. These two opposites collide most forcefully between the two parts; symbolically, this collision occurs on a narrow, shaky bridge, for the narrative link which connects the tale's two halves is no less precarious.[30]

Both farmers, Marti and his opponent, Manz, angrily leap onto the bridge from opposite banks of the stream; in the middle they meet, pummel each other in the face with their fists, and clinch in a wrestling match, each trying to dispatch his rival into the waters beneath the bridge. But just as Marti appears to be on the verge of succumbing to Manz and, therefore, of losing the curious battle of vengeance, the two children—Manz's son Sali and Marti's daughter Vrenchen—spontaneously enter the fray from opposite sides, hoping to aid their respective fathers. Nevertheless, Sali and Vrenchen's interests quickly collide with those of their embittered elders, for rather than succeeding in tipping the balance of the battle for or against either father, the boy, nineteen years old, and the girl, seventeen, at once become enraptured with one another. Just as suddenly they discover they have no interest whatsoever in the economic triumph of one family over the other. Stepping between the combatants, the two children break up the death match and simultaneously seal their affection for one another. Sali looks into Vrenchen's face, she gives him a quick smile, and before they part they clasp hands. The unseen beat of their hearts accomplishes just the opposite of what their fathers' bloodied fists had sought to do.

The tangible greed of the two peasants, which had become more and more consuming since the beginning of the tale, now withers away to the benefit of neither; the affections of Sali and Vrenchen, on the other hand, which have hardly been developed at all in the first part of the story, now suddenly mature into a blissful romance. The collision of the down-to-earth interests of Marti and Manz with the lofty romantic interests of their children—so vividly centered on a bridge between two opposite banks—changes the course of the narrative as suddenly and dramatically as the lightning which flashes above to illuminate the stormy clash on the darkened bridge below. The narrator could hardly have made it more strikingly clear that this confrontation constitutes the fulcrum of the seesaw balancing the two antiphonal parts of the novella.

Recurring alternation between the two forces is actually anticipated in miniature, yet in very impressive fashion, in the opening pages of the narrative, when we see Marti and Manz plowing the soil of their two fields in two opposite directions. As the one proceeds up the hill, the other moves downward on the other side. When the peak of the cap of the descending farmer tips forward over his brow, that of the ascending farmer falls back on his neck. The distinction constantly alternates between them, depending upon which direction they plow. All their actions from the beginning are strictly motivated by a genuine craving to make Mother Earth ever more productive, hence selfishly to increase their own material wealth. This basic greed is utterly divorced, by its very nature, from anything that could be called human, whether in an ethical or an aesthetic sense. For the two peasants, the only thing that matters is the augmentation of tangible possessions. The happiness and well-being of the other never enter into their calculations. Even the unlawful acquisition of property does not disturb their consciences.

Colliding directly with this opening narrative about the *sang froid* of the two sturdy landed proprietors is what appears to be another separate narrative interspersed throughout it: the romantic story of carefree happiness shared by the young children Vrenchen and Sali. The two stories mix no better than oil and water, each constantly competing with the other to attract the reader's attention. When the narrator sharpens his focus on the pastoral bliss of the children, the objective realism of the tillers of the soil drops from view; conversely, however, when the fathers' stark reality again returns to the forefront of the novella, the childhood idyll recedes into the background.

The two distinctive strands of narrative found in the first part of the novella—the realistic and the idealistic—are etched out in even bolder relief by the narrator's portrayal of the ground on which they take place. The emphasis on separate and distinctive fields delineating each of the two realms further helps to make evident the clash of opposites and the inevitable domination of the real over the ideal. The realm which has the most solid foundation is, of course, the farmland of the two humorless, hard-working men, land dedicated to no idle pleasures but only to the production of dividends from the earth and capital gains at the marketplace. Everything that is said about the men's real assets, and especially about their acquisitiveness in enlarging their own lands by encroaching on other land and enriching it by ridding it of stones, sharpens our appreciation of the hard facts of everyday life, of the real necessity of earning a livelihood in competitive society. At loggerheads with this very realistic world of workaday behavior is an idyllic world of make-believe located in between the two farmers' plowed fields, and therefore standing in the way of their efforts to expand their property. The narrator takes care to show how this middle realm seems devoid of reality, especially when it is contrasted with the other two properties. In the first place, it is covered with weeds and stones and is therefore unproductive. Second, it is nobody's legal possession, since the apparent owner, unable to prove his birth by a certificate or a reliable witness, has no birthright to the land he would otherwise inherit. Since he does not really exist—in the eyes

of the law—he has no valid claim to any real estate. Lacking a real
owner, the land is then left to be occupied by children at play, who,
with their unfettered imaginations, turn it into a paradisal world of
make-believe. It is a realm of irrational, childlike babblings, in-
nocent bliss, and romantic dreaming, as distant from workaday reality as are the farmers' lives from a delightful fairyland.

The two realms collide when the aggressive farmers plow their
way, furrow by furrow, into the primeval paradise situated between
their fields, and, above all, when they bid competitively to take
legal title to that ever-narrowing strip of land left to the whims of
weeds, rocks, and wild imagination in order to make it a source of
productivity. This will leave room neither for the children to indulge
in their bucolic play nor for the heir without proof to lay any further
claim to the property.

In the collision, the realm of the fictitious owner as well as of the
children's fantasy is smashed by the driving force of the fathers'
industriousness. As the heir is disenfranchised by the collision and
the children are expelled from their dreamlike playland, the fanciful
realm of the idyllic increasingly succumbs to the domination of
palpable reality. At the end of the novella's first part, all that seems
to matter is the sordid wrangling of the fathers for the acquisition
of material assets. The children's play and the claims of the fictitious
owner cease to be of further concern; the scale has clearly tipped
in favor of undisguised reality.

Now follows the crucial bridge episode mentioned earlier and
which constitutes the main fulcrum of the novella, for it completely
reverses the balance. The scale tips in the opposite direction, as
the world of reality recedes and the realm of imagination takes over.
The financial affairs and real estate of the fathers, so important in
the novella's first part, are now of less and less concern and gradually
vanish from view; and, conversely, the children's make-believe, no
longer limited to childish games blossoms into an enchanted love
affair.

After the great clash between the narrative's two extremes during
the bridge scene, the reader of the novella is led, metaphorically
speaking, across a bridge from the shore of reality into the land of
fantasy. Sali, we are told, loses sight of the real world about him
and transforms his old home—in his altered state of mind—into a
heavenly Jerusalem. The sense that the shore of the real world has
been left behind is further enhanced by the reader's knowledge that

Sali's father, having been forced to abandon his property, has now transferred his last resources to a squalid tavern which becomes a haven for thieves, the outcasts from society. Sali's mother, concurrently, has become a ludicrous figure in the estimation of those in full possession of their senses, for she seems more a part of the world of folly than of everyday Swiss existence. In their new home a pathetic form of comic relief dominates the descriptions. It is as though Sali's parents have become exiles from reality and found refuge on the clouds of the grotesque.

Vrenchen's father, too, has relinquished his real estate; in exchange, he takes up residence in a lunatic asylum where, now completely deprived of his reason, he becomes oblivious to the world around him. His imbecile antics offer the same comic relief that was present in the Manzes' tavern. Vrenchen's mother has also been banished from visible reality, though in her case at the hand of death.

We also notice at this stage of the novella that the real world is increasingly drawn into the world of make-believe. We are told of a peasant woman who believes both the invented story about Vrenchen and Sali's impending marriage and the equally fictive one about their newly acquired wealth. She has accepted the fabrications as true, thereby departing just as much from reality as have the young couple's parents. The same holds true for an innkeeper who is fooled by appearances and believes the lovers to be a rich couple, which they are not. In her gullibility she, too, mistakes fiction for reality and, as a result, is equally absorbed into the realm of the improbable.

The core of the novella's idyllic second half is the fairy-tale life of Vrenchen, appropriately referred to now as a princess, and that of her Prince Charming, Sali. With the sale of his silver watch, the keeper of real time, Sali signals the final abdication of the physical world in favor of a dream province. Having rid himself of this last remnant of reality, and with the proceeds he has received from its sale, he can now make a total commitment to the realm of make-believe. This commitment is highlighted by a mock wedding performed at a beautiful country locale fittingly named "The Garden of Paradise." Significantly, it is frequented by vagrants who have no actual home and whose state of inebriation has further put them out of touch with reality. The official who performs the marriage ceremony has, of all the characters in the novella, the least genuine

claim to do so: lacking a baptismal certificate and any secular proof
of his birth, he has neither a birthright to membership in the Christian community nor any official status as a citizen. In the eyes of
Church and State, the twin custodians of authority in the wedding
rite, the marrying official does not exist. The marriage, hence, is
null and void in society.

If this ceremony was performed in too irregular a fashion to enjoy
any legal recognition, the subsequent, bizarrely described wedding
procession transports the couple even farther away from normalcy,
for it is portrayed in a way that resembles the nocturnal procession
of a witches' sabbath. Later, the union is put even further at odds
with the institution of marriage when the carnivalistic betrothal is
sealed by counterfeit wedding rings.

Climaxing all this fantastic simulation of bourgeois joys, there
follows a nocturnal scene of mystic-romantic ecstasy aboard a hay-
barge set adrift in the middle of a river. As Sali carries his bride
onto the boat and unhitches it from its moorings, the narrator seems
to demonstrate once again that in this part of the novella all ties to
reality have been severed and cast aside. The mock marriage between the young dreamers having been consummated, a romantic
yearning for music, love, and death having been fulfilled, the two
lovers slip beneath the cold waters together. In such a romantic
death what is not possible in reality becomes possible. Yet even this
means that the two forces collide here in an imaginary sense as
much as they did at the bridge in a realistic sense.

This final collision of the real and the romantic is mirrored again
in the novella's anticlimactic epilogue, which Keller added in 1874.
We are told that the opinion shared by local pundits and arbiters
of the press—once daylight has again broken, reawakening harsh
reality and revealing the lovers' suicide—is one of shock and disgust.
The godforsaken nuptials of Vrenchen and Sali, their wanton shed-
ding of clothing, and their consequent departure from this life in
a state of utter nakedness (the Victorian critic George Henry Lewes
[1817–1878] once said the story could not be read by ladies![31])
clashed much too intensely, it seems, with the norms compatible
with the actual mores of the mid-nineteenth century. But which,
on the other hand, is truer to real life: the actual love affair of Sali
and Vrenchen or the pretended beliefs of the mid-nineteenth-century reading public?

Before we take leave of this compelling novella and turn our attention to another conspicuous representative of German Poetic Realism, it remains to be said that Keller further reinforced his poetic argument about the collision of the actual and the imaginative in the observable world by publishing this tale in a collection of novellas entitled *Die Leute von Seldwyla* (The People of Seldwyla). Seldwyla is a town which, according to the preface, is so real that it could be located anywhere in Switzerland. But it is also so fictitious that it can be found nowhere in Switzerland. It is unimaginable to conceive of a Swiss town in the life of which neither a church, school, nor marketplace plays a significant part, yet such is the case in *Romeo und Julia auf dem Dorfe*. The two Seldwylan characteristics obviously conflict with one another: if the town is real, it cannot be fictitious; and if it is fictitious, it cannot be real. By linking this novella, therefore, with a collection of stories bound together by the common feigned reality of Seldwyla, Keller reaffirms the tantalizing dichotomy for which he will forever be remembered.

III   *Conrad Ferdinand Meyer*

Conrad Ferdinand Meyer (1825–1898), another author from Zurich, was—unlike Storm and Keller—not one of the founding fathers of German Poetic Realism.[32] His calling to the literary movement came approximately thirty years after it had been ignited by the fires of 1848. Yet he came to occupy an exalted position in the movement; indeed, together with Storm and Keller he belongs to what may now be called the trinity of canonical novella-writers in German Poetic Realism.

The first to recognize that these three authors as a group towered over all other participants in the movement was the erudite editor of the literary monthly *Deutsche Rundschau,* Julius Rodenberg (1831–1914), a man who became singularly successful in promoting numerous works of the Poetic Realists through his widely circulating journal. Rodenberg granted Meyer the same extraordinary publication privilege which he had previously accorded only to Storm and Keller: each of the three could expect to have everything he wrote published in the *Deutsche Rundschau* immediately, without any further editorial approval.[33]

Other influential contemporary men of letters were also unequivocal in acknowledging the primacy of Storm, Keller, and Meyer at the apogee of German Poetic Realism. The versatile Prussian author and diplomat Rudolf Lindau (1829–1910), for instance, when asked in 1883 to name the best novella-writers at the time in the German-speaking world, promptly mentioned, as the first three, Keller, Meyer, and Storm.[34]

In spite of the fact, however, that Keller, Storm, and Meyer can be linked together in an auspicious trinity, there is a marked variation between the novellas of the earlier German Poetic Realists on the one hand and those of Meyer on the other. The former, baptized by the fires of revolution, had chosen their themes from everyday reality, whereas Meyer, writing thirty years later, passed over daily life to concentrate on historically remote subjects. This difference has prompted some modern critics, most notably E. K. Bennett, to dissociate Meyer from Poetic Realism altogether.[35] But such a separation fails to recognize the dynamic nature of that movement, which, like a powerful stream in its long course, can twist, turn, and strike out in different directions without losing its identity. If within this flux and flow the novellas of Storm and Keller exhibit an invigorating clarity of purpose because both authors were so close to the stream's source back in 1848, the novellas of Meyer possess a more exuberant vitality because they joined that same stream when it had become deeper, broader, and fuller. Hence, Storm and Keller may have had the advantage of being nearer the fountainhead of German Poetic Realism, but that advantage—important as it was—neither made them more typical representatives of the movement nor more perfect practitioners of its art than the latecomer Meyer.

No observer of literature has described Meyer's unique role in the literary movement after 1848 with more acuity, perception, and incisiveness than has the great apostle of German Poetic Realism himself, Julian Schmidt. It is one of the scandalous oversights of modern criticism that the ingenious essay in which Schmidt relates Meyer to the movement has been allowed to gather dust within the pages of the now-forgotten periodical *Preußische Jahrbücher*.[36] In this essay Schmidt shows conclusively that the difference between the contemporary themes of everyday reality chosen by the early German Poetic Realists and the historically remote themes of Meyer, rather than being an argument for separating Meyer from Storm and Keller, as Bennett later believed, actually constitutes an argument for linking them together and, moreover, for giving Meyer equal status as a towering figure. With extraordinary critical acumen Schmidt demonstrates that Meyer's stress on the past was not inconsistent with the realistic conception of literature derived from the revolutions, but was rather the logical and natural extension of the conception precisely at a time—thirty years after the revolutionary fires had cooled—when the movement's prolonged activity was impairing its former vigor. Far from corrupting the identity of Poetic Realism by his energetic thrust into the historical past, Meyer had—according to Schmidt—actually revitalized its original purpose and given it new life when it was in danger of dying of old age. For having thus rejuvenated Poetic Realism when it might otherwise have collapsed under its own weight, Meyer must be accorded a position of exceptional preeminence in the movement.

The details of Schmidt's argument are well worth resurrecting from the oblivion to which they have unfortunately been consigned. He begins by telling of the skepticism entertained by men of letters in the early days of German Poetic Realism with regard to all fiction that was historical in content. This was due to the fact that the Romantic poets had demonstrated a strong penchant for the remote corners of the past. The Romantics, after all, had taken a particular delight in yearning for "once upon a time," for being wafted away into enchanted realms far removed from reality. It goes without saying that "turning back the clock" in Romantic style was thoroughly repugnant to the early Poetic Realists. The turmoils of 1848–1849 had brought home to them that the affairs of the day, and not those of yesteryear, were what truly counted; hence they came to reject the kind of fiction which sent the mind wandering through the picture galleries of history. In its place they substituted a literature which had the arena of contemporary life as its concern.

However, after the movement had run its course for some years, Schmidt continues, the preoccupation with contemporary reality started to wear thin. The same subject matter taken from everyday life began to reappear in one work after the other, and—unavoidably—a fatal monotony set in. This prompted the more far-sighted Poetic Realists to search for themes less worn: these were found in history books. Real life could be rediscovered in actual records of the past and recast into story form. This broadened the dimensions of the movement, of course, in ways which would not have been conceivable earlier, when historical themes were taboo. Still, the purpose of Poetic Realism was not corrupted, for life in the past that actually happened was no less real than the life of the present.

But, as Schmidt points out, not all the Poetic Realists who turned to history were successful in translating into fiction the reality of the past, for, in the process, that reality was often lost sight of. Schmidt supports his argument by referring to the popular fiction of the talented contemporary Prussian Egyptologist Georg Ebers (1837–1898). As a writer who was also an authority on the Egyptian past, Ebers had a mind steeped in the history of the Nile Delta; and this historical knowledge supplied him with an impressive array of bedazzling themes for his stories. However, the reader is left with the feeling that these stories are no more than conventional tales of the present in picturesque Egyptian disguise. Ebers did justice to historical reality, Schmidt says, only by clothing modern characters in the colorful costumes of Ancient Egypt, by giving their language a touch of the obsolete, and by creating a stage setting reminiscent of the world around the Nile in antiquity. Ebers, therefore, did not portray the real life of Ancient Egypt; he merely feigned that reality.

Meyer's contribution to Poetic Realism stands out sharply against this background, for where Ebers and others did not succeed—or succeeded only in part—Meyer was spectacularly successful. His stories, as Schmidt convincingly shows, leave the reader with the distinct impression that the related events of the past actually occurred, and that the characters really lived. Furthermore, these episodes seem to illustrate those issues and men which really mattered in their day, those lives which actually shaped history.

Several years after the publication of Schmidt's essay, Otto Brahm (1856–1912), an influential critic in Naturalism, the literary movement that would eventually supersede Poetic Realism in Germany, was to say that Schmidt had gone overboard in his enthusiasm for Meyer.[37] But even this sobering comment merely reveals that—in the eyes of the man who had done so much to launch German Poetic Realism—a great author had now appeared on the scene to rejuvenate the movement at a time when the goals of the revolution had dropped from sight and, consequently, the sources of literary inspiration were running dry. Meyer, with his realistic historicism, had become not only a savior of the tired and stale movement, but, at the same time, the practitioner of a new and different variant of the only type of literature tolerated by its militant father.

Meyer made his impressive debut as a writer of novellas when

Der Heilige (The Saint) was published in three installments in the opening pages of the November and December 1879 and January 1880 issues of the *Deutsche Rundschau*. It was not, to be sure, the very first novella Meyer had written (nor was it to be the last), but it was certainly the one work which propelled him into the very forefront of German Poetic Realism. It was, above all, the novella which prompted Schmidt to write his *laudatio*. Indeed, Schmidt had hastened to acclaim Meyer for this novella so fast that his essay appeared in print even before the third installment of *Der Heilige* came off the press; and hardly had the printer's ink on the third installment dried than Schmidt once more began to extol this novella with all the superlatives at his command.[38] This was the novella, moreover, which won for Meyer the affection of Storm,[39] and which moved even Keller, who had never been too sympathetic to Meyer,[40] to admit, within just a few days of its publication, that his crosstown competitor had now written a truly splendid work.[41]

The praise of this novella spread most widely, however, when a young admirer of Julian Schmidt by the name of Johannes Haußleiter (1851–1928) wrote some highly laudatory comments in one of the most influential daily newspapers in the German-speaking world at the time, the *Allgemeine Zeitung*.[42] If Schmidt had skillfully drawn attention to the realistic qualities of Meyer's novellas, Haußleiter, with no less acumen, emphasized their dramatic qualities. Thus he reminded the reader that Meyer's novellas, in addition to aligning fiction with realism, allow another cardinal principle of the novella of German Poetic Realism to remain dominant: that that genre should be, as Storm stipulated, a prosaic "sister of the drama."

Schmidt, it is only fair to state, had also pointed to the dramatic life of Meyer's important novellas,[43] but his first concern had been to show how consonant their historic realism was with the requirements of Poetic Realism. Thus it remained for the younger Haußleiter to develop this other thought further, and he accomplished the task by focusing attention on the particular novella which he, too, felt to be Meyer's most outstanding achievement: *Der Heilige*. It is interesting to note that Meyer, after having read Haußleiter's analysis of *Der Heilige*, singled it out as being particularly excellent.[44] We know, therefore, how Meyer liked his novella to be read. Today, unfortunately, Haußleiter's essay—like the commentaries of Julian Schmidt—has been forgotten; but, like Schmidt's essays, it deserves a better fate, not least of all because Meyer himself thought so highly of it.

Schmidt's junior comrade-in-arms makes it clear that the drama in *Der Heilige* is a conflict between man's temporal and eternal values, between the concerns of a mortal body and the salvation of an immortal soul; it is one between civil power and sacerdotal jurisdiction, between the competency of a secularly oriented State and the mission of a divinely inspired Church. It is, in particular, a clash which history has recorded as having been present in the conflict of loyalties within Thomas à Becket, the twelfth-century English politician who was raised to sainthood in the Catholic Church. As soon as the historic reality of Becket appears in the novella, as soon as his contradictory personality is reanimated for the reader, an inherent drama is present. We see Becket first as Chancellor of England and later as Archbishop of Canterbury, first as the chief aide to the despotic King Henry II of England and later as the primate of the King whose kingdom is "not of this world."

In his early role, Becket, with little apparent regard for right or wrong, zealously strives to strengthen and uphold royal power, frequently at the expense of ecclesiastical prerogatives. He appears first as an ardent and dutiful abettor of a tyrannical Caesarism bent on reducing everything—specifically, however, the Church—to a state of submission to the Crown of England.

The Church, history tells us, constituted the most formidable obstacle to the royal supremacy of Henry II. It insisted on preemptory rights in the jurisdiction of the clergy and would not tolerate the substitution of any civil courts of appeal for legal matters involving a member of the clergy (and their number was large). It likewise insisted on its divine right of sole jurisdiction in all matters pertaining to Christian matrimony and to the tables of consanguinity derived from marriage; thereby it also possessed an exclusive jurisdiction over all matters related to inheritance. In short, the Church's power within the internal order of the State was considerable, and the cause of great irritation to a king trying to exercise absolute authority. Rubbing even more salt into the wound, the Church's power was controlled by a foreign ruler, the Pope in Rome. King Henry counted on his able chancellor to help him curb this papal interference in English affairs, but he knew that his purpose could only be attained after a hard contest. Only a few decades earlier the Pope had humbled the German emperor at Canossa: the world had seen the spectacle of a mighty emperor prostrate in the dust before an almost supernatural "Vicar of Christ." The scene of papal triumph had dazzled the imagination of Europe and had set the tiara scintillating with a brilliance never seen before.

As Meyer relates in *Der Heilige*, Henry chose well his time to act: a new Pope on the throne of St. Peter had a passion for augmenting the Vatican's royal coffers; it could safely be assumed, therefore, that he would not easily offend any sovereign from whom he received supplies of money. This left only the Catholic "Primate of All England," the Archbishop of Canterbury, as the source of any effective ecclesiastical opposition. Most cunningly, Henry causes his faithful friend and pliant advocate of his policies, Becket, to be elected to the Archbishopric of Canterbury. No more perfect political scheme could be imagined to bring about the total submission of the Church to the State, and Becket is the chief instrument in the plan.

Now the second aspect of Becket's historically documented, contradictory personality comes into focus. The former chancellor of the English king and willing tool of secular power, once installed in the archiepiscopal See of Canterbury as the chief "Vicar of Christ" in England, becomes just as faithful and tenacious in his service to his divine Master as he had been formerly in his dedication to the interests of his earthly sovereign. Becket now takes exactly the opposite stance from the one he had previously taken in the struggle between secular and spiritual power. To the astonishment of everyone—but most of all to that of King Henry—the luxury- and splendor-loving Becket suddenly casts aside all interest in worldly riches and chooses to go about in the raiment of penance followed by a motley crowd of beggars, sick, lame, and blind, whom he now invites to dine at his table in place of the retinue of noble lords who were his former guests. The king's most dutiful servant now becomes a highly militant advocate of spiritual power, or, as Hauß-leiter puts it, "more popish than the Pope." In the ensuing battle with his earthly sovereign, Becket soon suffers the death of a martyr for the Church, in no less exalted a place than before the high altar of Canterbury Cathedral.

This crown of martyrdom gives Becket the ultimate victory, for it causes Henry's throne to crumble, and Henry himself is compelled to prostrate and scourge himself at the tomb of his erstwhile ecclesiastical adversary, who has since been canonized. Hence, the dramatic forces have completely reversed themselves: where at first royal supremacy had trampled over everything spiritual, with Becket as the most able bearer of the king's scepter, now it is the divine glow of the Church, with Becket as its most invincible tool of retribution, which triumphs over the material world of the State.

But if, as Haußleiter argues, the historically documented record of Becket, so authentically incorporated into the novella, contains the essential drama of the two contradictory forces governing human life, it is nevertheless the particular accomplishment of Meyer as a novella-writer that makes this drama come alive. Meyer goes beyond the facts of history books and relates Becket's story as it is "remembered" by a friend of Becket whom Meyer invents for his fictional purpose. This poetic device gives the author an advantage not enjoyed by the objective historian, who can only record, without adornment, what really took place in Becket's life. At Meyer's touch, historical reality is suffused with poetic fantasy in such a way that on the very day the Church recognizes Becket's eternal membership in the incorruptible company of celestial hosts, the enfeebled mind of a simple tradesman by the name of Hans gives a personalized account of the events occurring during Becket's terrestrial existence. Throughout the portrayal of the real life of the saint, the reader is never allowed to forget that he is listening to a manufactured and often amusing version of the actual story of Becket. Fiction and history thus dovetail; the two elements interpenetrate, amplifying one another and further serving to support the human conflict on which this novella is built.

The poetically invented story of Hans enables the saint to appear as a real person before the eyes of the reader; yet at the same time the divinely conceived union of sin and sanctity which gave Becket his extraordinary qualities contrasts all the more vividly with the naturalistically described, very real and down-to-earth experiences of the simple-minded Hans. Occasionally the reader wonders which character is more concrete, Hans or Becket; which story is more real, the narrative of Hans referring to fact but only recording a fictive opinion, or the historically authenticated story of the saint which comes alive for us when portrayed by a fictional character who has ostensibly enjoyed his personal confidence? Essentially, however, it makes no difference, for Meyer intends the inseparability of the two conflicting forces found in the actual historical figure to be no less visible in the interlacing of the natural and supernatural which characterizes the whole of his fictional enterprise.

CHAPTER 3

The Lyric

I The Anthologies

A LARGE number of richly varied, competing anthologies of German verse appeared in print during the age of German Poetic Realism, bringing in a bountiful harvest of contemporary lyric poetry. But the reception accorded to the new movement's poetry by the truly critical anthologists of the day quickly winnowed the copious crop of verse and pointed to those lyricists who were to constitute its permanent canon.

Theodor Fontane, who, next to Julian Schmidt, must be considered the most astute literary critic in Germany during the second half of the nineteenth century, was also the most conspicuous anthologist to survey and assess the new German verse soon after the pivotal year 1848. Fontane's anthology was, to be sure, not the first one to emerge after the revolutions. That distinction belongs to the third edition of *Album deutscher Dichter,* compiled in 1849 by Hermann Kletke (1813–1886). But Kletke's volume was too conservative to be representative of the new age. Fontane's anthology, on the other hand—entitled *Deutsches Dichteralbum* and initially published in 1852—distinctly reflected the new mood. It sold rapidly; one edition quickly followed another. Within ten years after the barricades had been removed from the streets of Berlin, the fourth edition was on display in the windows of that city's bookshops. This anthology—perhaps as its most salutary feature—sought to awaken its readers to a new sense of literary appreciation by placing a new poem of Theodor Storm on the opening page. In this manner, Storm was thrust into the very forefront of postrevolutionary poetry. Furthermore, as if to make doubly sure that the readers understood Storm to be the outstanding poet of the day, Fontane saw to it that

56

his lyric voice resounded louder than that of any other post-1848 poet.

Fontane also assigned a commanding position to another budding voice of German Poetic Realism, the Low German poet Klaus Groth (1819–1899). The first three editions of *Deutsches Dichteralbum* contained none of Groth's poems, whose name was not even mentioned. But the fourth edition, appearing in 1858, brought about a dramatic change. Fontane modified his selection in such a way that Groth became the second strongest representative of the new movement. In his preface to the fourth edition, moreover, Fontane called particular attention to the intrinsic value of Groth's poems, stating that they were being added to the anthology at the expense of poems by others with less merit. Thus Groth became—in Fontane's opinion—the second chief exponent of the new type of verse which arose out of the ashes of 1848.

About the same time that Fontane was at work gathering and sorting out the lyrics of German Poetic Realism, a Swabian professor of aesthetics by the name of Georg Scherer (1824–1909) also began to collect and establish the canon of what he considered to be the best of the new movement's poetry. Five years after the 1848 revolutions, Scherer edited his critical anthology of contemporary German verse, *Deutscher Dichterwald*, whose title made it an immediate rival of Fontane's anthology. In its many subsequent reprints and revisions, it became the successor to Fontane's anthology as the principal forum for the German verse of Poetic Realism. Fontane discontinued his careful sifting of newly published poetry after 1858, while Scherer continued to review critically and to compile the verse of his contemporaries for another half-century.

Scherer's opinion of what constituted the canon of Poetic Realism's poetry became, perhaps, most evident in the handsomely illustrated sixteenth edition of his anthology. It appeared in 1894, soon after the movement had drawn to a close and at a time when all that the age had produced in the realm of the lyric was known to Scherer. (His personal library, now a part of the Bayerische Staatsbibliothek in Munich, contains one of the most extensive collections of contemporary poetry in existence at the time.)

Scherer states in the preface to his work that he intends to offer a complete survey of modern German poetry; and, indeed, no other nineteenth-century anthology ranges over such a broad area of German verse of the age as his volume. This claim of historic completeness did not mean for Scherer, of course, that all the modern poets deserved to receive equal coverage. It is instructive today to look back and note how this erudite critic sorted out the verse of his time, highlighting some poets more than others.

Following the pattern established by Fontane, Scherer accorded to Storm, twelve of whose poems are included in the collection, the undisputed primacy among the lyricists of German Poetic Realism. None of the other voices rings out nearly so loudly. After Storm—again as if Scherer were continuing Fontane's tradition—comes Klaus Groth with seven poems. Tying with Groth for second place, however—and this is a novelty in Scherer's collection—is Conrad Ferdinand Meyer, likewise represented with seven poems. A further novelty of Scherer's anthology, in contrast to Fontane's, is the addition of verse by Keller. Fontane had conspicuously omitted Keller's lyrics, but Scherer, printing five poems by Keller, granted to this Swiss author a place of importance among the poets of Poetic Realism. Storm, Groth, Meyer, and Keller thus became the four noteworthy lyricists of the age in Scherer's estimation. Other poets of the movement were merely given token representation for the sake of historic completeness.

Scherer was not entirely without rival. Echtermeyer's *Auswahl deutscher Gedichte,* named after its original compiler, Theodor Echtermeyer (1805–1844), constitutes another impressive critical anthology of German verse, appearing in one successive—and successful—edition after the other throughout the age. In contrast to Fontane and Scherer's volumes, however, this widely read anthology places more emphasis, particularly in its earlier editions, on German Classical Poetry. Nevertheless, succeeding editions gradually offered an ever-increasing number of selections from modern German verse. Beginning with the ninth edition of 1856, for instance, Groth's poetry is given a special place of prominence. For the reception of Poetic Realism the thirtieth edition, compiled by Hermann Masius (1818–1893), a distinguished professor in Leipzig, contains the most revealing selections. This edition, published in 1891, came out—like Scherer's of 1894—when all of what German Poetic Realism had produced in poetry was available for critical inspection. Of the movement's poetry, Storm's received the heaviest accent in this volume, with no fewer than nine of his poems being reprinted. The attention given to Storm is all the more conspicuous when compared to the lesser amount of space apportioned to such recognized earlier masters of German verse as Annette von Droste-Hülshoff, Joseph von Eichendorff, or Heinrich Heine. The second most conspicuous lyricist of Poetic Realism in the 1891 Masius edition of Echtermeyer's anthology is—again—Klaus Groth. He trails Storm; but with five poems to his credit he is made to outrank any of the other Poetic Realists in importance.

The early critical reception of the movement's verse is rounded out by two further anthologies. The first of these is the *Hausbuch aus deutschen Dichtern seit Claudius*, compiled by none other than Theodor Storm. It first appeared in 1870, and three subsequent editions quickly followed within the same decade. The volume contains verse from poets whose roots are anchored in the eighteenth century, notably Matthias Claudius, but the main emphasis is plainly placed on more modern verse. Many Poetic Realists, particularly Storm himself, are represented. The handsomely illustrated 1875 edition, for instance, contains nine of his own poems. More revealing, though, is the fact that Storm accentuates Groth's poetry just as strongly as he does his own. Groth and Storm shine forth from the pages of the *Hausbuch aus deutschen Dichtern seit Claudius* as the two outstanding lyricists of Poetic Realism. Keller, on the other hand, occupies a much weaker position with only three entries; and Meyer does not appear at all. If the most remarkable feature in Storm's selection of contemporary poetry is the highly favorable light in which he regards Groth's verse, the striking characteristic of an anthology entitled simply *Die deutsche Lyrik der Gegenwart*, compiled in 1884 by the Viennese literary critic Fritz Lemmermayer (1857–1932), is the top ranking it confers on Keller. In this anthology, Keller is regarded as the strongest lyric representative of Poetic Realism, but Storm and Meyer also loom large. The other lyric voices of the movement, by comparison, are given far less space.

The anthologies of Lemmermayer, Storm, Echtermeyer-Masius, Scherer, and Fontane, besides helping to gain wider audiences for the best of the poetry of Poetic Realism, were the important critical forums of the day as well. But there were, of course, a host of other anthologies seeking to capitalize on the tremendous contemporary interest in lyric poetry and to popularize the new verse. Most of these, however, tended to be indiscriminate in the selections of verse they offered. Often enough they lacked the evaluative yardstick that is the mark of a critical anthology; and, as a result, such collections more frequently resemble over-extensive jumbles than critical attempts to establish the permanent canon of the poetry of Poetic Realism. Even highly popular, best-selling anthologies of new poetry like Elise Polko's *Dichtergrüße, Neuere deutsche Lyrik* (1860), Rudolf Gottschall's *Blüthenkranz neuer deutscher Dichtung* (1870), and Ferdinand Avenarius's *Deutsche Lyrik der Gegenwart seit 1850* (1882) scarcely constitute more than hurried attempts to appease the verse-hungry appetites of large segments of the populace and make little distinction between good and bad poetry. Gottschall and Avenarius's anthologies, most particularly, lack critical standards. Gottschall possessed, in the opinion of no lesser critic than Julian Schmidt, a remarkable insensitivity to what is intimately poetic.[1] As for Avenarius, both Keller and Storm were in complete agreement that he could not tell a good poem from a bad one.[2]

All the more important, of course, were the truly critical anthologies. Almost without exception they made it clear that Storm was held in esteem as the foremost lyricist after the middle of the nineteenth century. Critical opinion differed as to the further rankings of Groth, Keller, and Meyer in their positions next to Storm. But that these three poets, together with Storm, had left an indelible mark on the shaping of the poetry of the age, there can be no doubt.

II *Theodor Storm*

As with the novella of German Poetic Realism, so too with the lyric genre: Storm enjoys the distinction of coming earliest. Not unnaturally, his development into the first major lyricist of the new literary movement paralleled the path he followed when emerging as its first important novella-writer.

In Storm's formative years, while he was still a loyal subject of the Danish Crown, he had become thoroughly conversant with the lyrical mood prevailing in Denmark. By 1843, he had been able to demonstrate before a representative of the Crown that he could translate Danish verse into German with both skill and ease.[3] The poetry of his "Danish" period closely follows the tone of Danish poetry at the time. In fact, the same musical quality that Julian Schmidt had found to be characteristic of Danish verse of his day[4] typifies Storm's early poems as well. Essentially, they reverberate with song; above all, they emphasize rhyme and sound effects.

Pictures and images are sacrificed to mood, as they dissolve into a melodious play of consonants and vowels.

An exquisite example of such an orchestration of rhyme and sound is Storm's poem "An die Entfernte M." (To M., Who Is Far Away). Storm wrote this poem in 1835, but it did not appear in print— curiously enough—until Storm's biographer Franz Stuckert published it in 1955.[5] More recently, it has found its way into print again in the collection of Storm's works edited by Peter Goldammer.[6] In both instances, however, the text has been garbled and the poem's musical rhythm distorted. We quote the poem, therefore, as recorded in Storm's own handwriting on page twenty-eight of a little bound volume entitled *Meine Gedichte*, now in the possession of the library of the Theodor Storm Society in Husum:

> Eilende Winde
> Wieget Euch linde
> Säuselt mein Liebchen der Lieblichen vor;
> Vögelein singet,
> Vögelein bringet
> Töne der Lust an ihr lauschendes Ohr!
> Öffne dich Rose,
> Schwellet ihr Moose,
> Reiht Euch ihr Blumen zum duftigen Strauß;
> Weilt ihr am Herzen,
> Horcht ihren Scherzen,
> Bannet den trübenden Kummer hinaus.
> Schimmernde Sterne,
> Strahlt aus der Ferne
> Himmlischer Höhen ihr Freude u. Lust,
> Freundliche Sterne
> Wärt ihr nicht ferne
> Leuchtet ihr tröstend d. liebende[n] Brust.

> (Hurrying winds
> Cradle gently,
> Whisper this song to my beloved;
> Birds, sing,
> Birds, bring
> Sounds of pleasure to her listening ear!
> Open yourself, rose,
> Rise up, you mosses,
> Gather yourselves, flowers, into a sweet-smelling bouquet;

Linger at her heart,
Listen to her jests,
Banish gloomy sorrow,
Shimmering stars,
Shine down joy and delight to her
From afar off on heavenly heights,
Kindly stars
If you weren't so far off
You could give light, comfortingly, to her loving breast.)

Translated by Richard D. Hacken

Verses like these typify a poetry sealed off from actuality. The words serve primarily as musical notes and hardly relate to the objects they are supposed to identify. Far overshadowing the content, the tonal effects echo luscious rhythm in the many dancing lines and seem to ring out like dazzling choruses in the lilting rhyme schemes. There is little time to pause and little that is worthy of pause; everything seems subordinate to the auditory appeal of exhilarating acoustic melody. So all-important is the music of this poem (and so unimportant its content, syntax, and grammar) that individual portions could be interchanged without destroying any coherence or meaning. The poem thus constitutes a verbal equivalent of music, conveying a sense of intoxication with the musical qualities of language and revealing Storm—like many of his Danish contemporaries—primarily as a poet for the ear. It is hardly a coincidence that the poem's exhilarating rhythm reminds us of the all-pervading birdlike melody that gives Hans Christian Andersen's "Gurre" (written in 1842) its buoyant power. Storm is composing here, rather obviously, within the orbit of contemporary Danish verse-melody.

But if it can be said that inner life became articulate as a result of inherent musical tones in the poetry of Storm's "Danish" period, it must also be noted that Storm abandoned this conception of poetry when the revolutions came. The blood spilled all around him from 1848 until 1850 forced the pervasive musical tradition of the Danish lyric to wane in his writing and made it impossible for him to continue writing verse in the same lilting tones as before. Now he became infected by the more vivid, down-to-earth quality of the political poetry which had suddenly taken root in the south, in Germany. Storm now wrote political lyrics in which topical issues prevailed. In these patently realistic poems he demonstrated his desire to come to grips with the political reality of the German minority revolt within the Danish kingdom. Gone were the strains of vagueness so characteristic of Storm's prerevolutionary verse; in their place arose a new descriptive art spelling out specific situations that politically affected the lives of citizens in the world close to him.

"Gräber an der Küste" (Graves on the Coast) is Storm's most poignant political poem. First written in October 1850, it shows the poet's immediate response to the most gruesome scene he had encountered in the insurrections about him: the final crushing of the local rebellion by the troops of the Danish Crown on October 4, 1850, at Friedrichstadt, a few miles south of his native Husum. Over 700 soldiers of the revolutionary militia had been killed in this last desperate attempt of the insurgents to free themselves from the yoke of Denmark. Storm despaired as much over the catastrophic loss of human life as over the lost cause he had supported. It was in this moment of despondent political passion, at a time of personally felt crisis, that he composed this poem, which is also an account of the reality of the day. Almost as if in diametric contrast to "An die Entfernte M.," which seems to be sealed off from actuality, this new poem offers vivid imagery provoked by political reality. Particularly exemplary of Storm's new penchant for a clarity of outline is the sixth stanza, written only three weeks after the rebels' defeat:

> Unwillig muß die wilde Dannebrog
> An eurer Gruft das Ehrenamt verwalten;
> Ihr zwangt den Feind, der euch hinunterzog,
> Sein Banner bei den Todten zu entfalten. [7]

> (Unwillingly must the wild Danish flag
> Be the guard of honor at your tomb;
> You forced the enemy who dragged you down
> To unfurl his banner among the dead.)

> *Translated by A. Tilo Alt* [8]

The somberness of this stanza strongly contrasts with the florid decoration of dancing melody which had given form to the poem "An die Entfernte M."; neither rhyme nor rhythm are important now; what counts is the visual reference to a specific historic content:

the unfurling of the flag of the Danish victors at the tomb of the
rebel war-dead, and the satisfaction of the vanquished that, by
dying, they may have scored the final victory. If the poem "An die
Entfernte M." is musical, "Gräber an der Küste" is pictorial; if the
earlier poem constitutes a dazzling sound melody, this one seeks
to produce an austere, almost photographically realized vignette;
if formerly content was subordinated to rhyme and rhythm, now
rhyme and rhythm are subordinated to content. Storm, the poet
for the ear, has been replaced by Storm, the poet for the eye. The
poet of Danish romanticism in happier days has become the poet
of German realism as a result of the German insurrections against
the Danes.

Yet, as we have said earlier when referring to Storm's development as a novella-writer, he still—for all his interest in realism—
remained indebted to Danish romanticism. Thirty years of citizenship in the Danish monarchy and an intimate familiarity with the
musical tradition of Danish literature had left an indelible mark on
Storm. Much as the revolution against the Danish Crown provoked
him to embrace the new, more realistic political literature that had
suddenly sprung up in Germany, he could not succumb for long to
this enticement. His roots in the literary climate of Denmark prevented him from being swept completely away by the new form of
German poetry.

A whole series of revisions which Storm made of "Gräber an der
Küste" during the years immediately following its first draft are
eloquent testimony to his increasing desire to resist the temptation
of turning verse into a political forum. The poem, first written as
his immediate response to the bloody scene at Friedrichstadt,
turned out to be so stained with political invective that he took great
pains, in subsequent revisions, to rid it of its most tendentious
aspects. Some of the most savage political strokes which he had first
angrily dashed onto paper were gradually eliminated. In each of the
subsequent revisions he sought to reduce the astringent content
further (the above-mentioned sixth stanza was eventually struck
from the poem altogether); and the specific historical references
were ultimately replaced by what he considered to be more enduring lyric qualities.[9]

So Storm turned away again from the boldly descriptive political
lyric which he had so quickly—all too quickly—embraced in the
heat of the insurrections. Nevertheless, he had become so severely

infected by "the scarlet fever of the blood-red lyric of liberation," as Rudolf Gottschall (1823–1909) called it,[10] that he could not feel entirely comfortable writing verse of the kind he had produced in prerevolutionary days. If he wanted to continue writing poetry, of course, this left him with no alternative but to blaze a new trail in the art of verse-writing. The resultant lyric style synthesized what he had imbibed while still composing in the sphere of Danish verse-melody and what he subsequently learned from the descriptive realism of the new German political poetry of 1848. One could say that Storm grafted the melodious lyre of the Danish muse onto the unflinching vision of the concrete that was inherent in German revolutionary poetry. Musical emotion was thus united with a clarity of outline, and an extraordinary fusion of the musical with the visual occurred. The thought-provoking verse born out of the marriage of these two sensory realms made Storm the first major lyricist of German Poetic Realism.

The first collection of Storm's poems published after he had learned how to blend successfully auditory and visual appeal in verse bore the simple title *Gedichte*. It appeared in 1852. However, this volume, containing some of Storm's finest postrevolutionary poetry, did not appeal to the mood of the new age in German literature in the same spectacular way in which Storm's post-1848 prose fiction (notably *Immensee*) had succeeded in captivating the new reading public. This is not surprising, since Storm made the unwise decision to include in the *Gedichte* both his pre- and his postrevolutionary verse. The collection was, therefore, not completely in tune with Poetic Realism. In each subsequent edition of the *Gedichte* (the seventh and final edition appeared in 1885), Storm repeated the same blunder. Gems of Poetic Realism were interspersed among lesser poems, composed before the perfection of his new style. Storm was, of course, well aware that he had committed an error in including these two dissimilar forms of verse in one volume. He confessed his mistake to the poet Eduard Mörike (1804–1875). Even though he knew he had made an unwise decision, he felt—as he told Mörike—that he could not disown his early poems.[11]

But if Storm's book of poetry, because of its unfortunate admixture, did not have the same appeal to the taste of the literary public after 1848 as the novellas had, this does not mean that the volume contained no masterpieces of Poetic Realism. Nothing could have

attested more eloquently to Storm's genius as a new lyricist than
the prominence given to his verse in Fontane's *Deutsches Dichter-
album.* The new poetic movement had hardly become established
when Fontane accorded Storm a position of primacy in it. But
Fontane's attempt to identify Storm as the most outstanding of the
new lyrical talents did not end at this point. As time progressed,
that astute critic could no longer content himself with placing Storm
solely at the head of the movement's early lyrical exponents. The
more Fontane became acquainted with the entire range of poetry
in the second half of the nineteenth century, the more he became
convinced that Storm's poetry possessed qualities superior to everything the entire age was producing in the realm of lyric poetry.
This, of course, echoed the belief held by most critical anthologists
in Germany at that time; yet none of these had voiced the opinion
as incisively or as ardently as had Fontane. "Ten lines of Storm's
verse," Fontane commented in 1883, "outweigh the entire annual
production of all those who presently reign supreme as champions
of the lyric."[12] In 1888—the year of Storm's death—Fontane came
to the conclusion that Storm was "the finest lyricist Germany had
produced since Goethe."[13] One year later, in 1889, he went one
step further by saying that Storm's lyrics were "equal in quality to
the very best ever written" in the German language.[14]

More recently, none other than Thomas Mann has corroborated
Fontane's judgment. Referring to Storm's poetry, Mann said:

In this ten times sorted and sifted lyrical treasure, gem stands almost next
to gem. There is a constant, thrilling, concentrated power of expression
about life and the emotions, a skill at shaping in the simplest form, which
in certain poems—however old you are, however often you read them—
unfailingly bring the catch in the throat as you are seized by that sweet
and ruthless and woeful sense of life. . . . at least half a dozen [of Storm's
poems] are worthy to stand beside the best and highest in feeling and
language and possess the unmistakable traits of immortality.[15]

Of these half-dozen poems considered by Mann to be immortal,
none has established itself with more persistence in one anthology
after the other, from the middle of the nineteenth century onward,
than has "Meeresstrand" (Seashore). Published for the first time in
1856 in the second edition of Storm's *Gedichte*, it was the only one
in the group which Storm himself deemed worthy of being included

in his highly exclusive anthology, *Hausbuch aus deutschen Dichtern seit Claudius.* When the noted Swedish poet and critic Anders Österling (b. 1884) once sought to bring Storm's verse to the attention of a larger audience in Sweden, this was the very first poem he chose to discuss.[16] Manfred Hausmann, a contemporary German poet, has ranked it among the ten most beautiful poems ever composed in the German language:[17]

> Ans Haff nun fliegt die Möwe,
> Und Dämmrung bricht herein;
> Über die feuchten Watten
> Spiegelt der Abendschein.
>
> Graues Geflügel huschet
> Neben dem Wasser her;
> Wie Träume liegen die Inseln
> Im Nebel auf dem Meer.
>
> Ich höre des gärenden Schlammes
> Geheimnisvollen Ton,
> Einsames Vogelrufen—
> So war es immer schon.
>
> Noch einmal schauert leise
> Und schweiget dann der Wind;
> Vernehmlich werden die Stimmen,
> Die über der Tiefe sind.[18]

> (The gull now flies to the harbor,
> the reddening sun sinks low,
> the sea beyond the marshes
> reflects the evening glow.
>
> Gray water-fowl are skimming
> the surface as they flee,
> as dreams the islands hover
> in mists upon the sea.
>
> I hear the seething marshes'
> mysterious sounds again,
> strange and lonesome bird cries—
> so it has always been.
>
> Once more a breath comes trembling,

and then the breezes sleep,
and one can hear the voices
that move above the deep.)

Translated by J. W. Thomas[19]

At its more obvious biographical level, "Meeresstrand" reflects Storm's mood of despondency arising ultimately from his acquaintance with the horrors of war, the lost political cause, and his exile in a strange land. Nostalgically, the poem seeks out the seaside town Storm fled after it had fallen into the hands of the royalist troops. Storm, exiled far from the sea, evokes images and sounds of his lost seaside homeland. The vividness of his native shorescape shows the poet's acute sensitivity to reality. Though they are physically remote, he still sees the wet mud flats and the fog-shrouded islands beyond; and though their sounds are no longer audible, he distinctly hears the sharp cry of the seagull and clearly perceives the never-varying flow of the tides.

Above all, Storm notices the process of annihilation to which all life is subject, and from which, he senses, no escape is possible. Was Storm predicting that his native shore, now held by the royalist enemy, would somehow perish? Or was he foreseeing an even more complete annihilation from destructive flood tides loosed in fury by an incomprehensible force from the unknown beyond? In his utter despair, both thoughts doubtlessly merged. Annihilation raged in his blood like an obsessive passion, and passed into his verse as a transfiguring element: as a result, he created a depressing, elegiac dirge of life's evanescence.

The poem consists of two equal halves. The first two stanzas rely on visual stimuli: the poet sees the last gull seeking evening refuge in the harbor as the light of day departs, and he sees the eventide fall over the desolate expanse of mud flats made bare by ebb-tide. Then the darkness deepens; things perceived with the eye grow dimmer. The seagull, which the poet saw so clearly in the gathering twilight of the first stanza, is replaced in the second stanza by more blurred, faded images: gray wings (presumably still of seagulls) scurrying indistinctly along the shore, and the wavering contours of islands dying away in the fog upon the horizon.

The last two stanzas, juxtaposed to the first two, appeal to the ear rather than the eye. The descending darkness has fully shrouded the earth and the sea, and all things visible have passed from view.

The poet can only hear the bubbling of the water caused by de-composing organic life in the ooze, and the last call of life uttered by a lonely bird still awake (still alive?). A curious dash now follows in the poem—indicating, like a musical *fermata*, a hold or pause. The mysterious sound of decay and the chilling shriek of the gull linger on in the darkness beyond their given time values and, in a bar of full rest, let the sting of death penetrate, with a harrowing sensation, into the ear. It is the abiding message of passing time. A shudder of the wind makes itself heard before it, too, finally dies down after the hours have fully run, signaling the end of day. Then comes the poem's grand finale: the ghostly foes ensconced in night, the sinister voices of nocturnal fears and fantasies, all join together in one last unending chorus.

Pinpointed precisely in the middle of this song of confrontation between life and death, imprisoned smack in its center, is an ele-ment of extreme personal involvement: the *ich*. Occurring, signif-icantly, as the first word of the third stanza, this lone first person is caught at the intersection of the poem's visual and acoustic halves; it is, moreover, deeply anchored at this point by virtue of its being in the poem's heaviest line (nine syllables). The *ich* is irretrievably entrapped, therefore, within the gruesome sights and sounds of transience, forever bound to their collage of decay, no less subject to the inevitable process of change than is the shore to the perpetual motion of the tides.

Firmly anchored in the center of the poem, man—with a heavy heart—is compelled to witness with his senses how night descends all around him. He sees the light of his day slowly but surely falling into the shadows, and then, as the light vanishes, his ears remind him that all semblances of permanency are ebbing away. First, he hears a final outcry in the gloom and then the deathly silence which occurs when the last breath of wind has brought the day of his life to its appointed end—from cradle to grave. Nothing remains astir save those mysterious voices beyond the grave which humans can hear only because the life of the everyday world no longer inter-poses.

Centrally located in the ninth line of the poem, man not only sees and hears how life and death interlock about him, but finds himself teased and haunted by the echoing dualities of the song as well. For the entire aria of transience is plentifully garnished with acoustic effects which constantly reecho man's life-death struggle.

In particular, the height and depth of the vowels reiterate this. In the poem's first line, the vowels are first muffled or low-pitched (*Ans Haff nun*) and then become high-pitched (*fliegt die Möwe*). Moving back down the scale at the beginning of the second line, they are muffled once more (*Und Dämmrung*); at the end of that line they ascend again to the high pitch (*bricht herein*). In counterpoint fashion, the second two lines make the reverse audible: in a descending order, the high-pitched vowels at the beginning of both lines (*Über die; Spiegelt der*) contrast sharply with the sounds at the end of the lines, where the vowels first fall precipitously, and then rise again (*feuchten Watten; Abendschein*). This effect, carried throughout the stanzas in various interplays, not only gives a rich orchestral coloration to the poem, but also reflects the interwoven character of life and death. The purest concentration of equally pitched vowels resounds in the last two lines, as a final orchestral fusion seems to occur between the previously alternating highs of life and lows of the grave. The heart monitor—to use a modern medical analogy—seems to be leveling off to an ominous hum. Yet vowel height is not the only form of orchestral reinforcement; the brevity of time and the length of bleak eternity are hammered into the auditory senses by the metrical beat as well. The steady series of iambs in the song's first two lines reiterate this no less than the equally steady series of trochees in the second half of the first stanza. The final stanza repeats the metrical rhythm of the opening one, and together these two stanzas enclose the vibrating life of more polyphonic metrics immediately surrounding man in the central two stanzas. The low tide of man's life at the beginning and at the end— at birth and at death—encloses the high tide of his active life in between.

All in all, the poem offers a disquieting meditation on the reality of the human destiny. Man is confronted with a somber script of his life's cycle, with the four "seasons" of his short "year" on earth— as the poem's four stanzas would metaphorically suggest—with a life which knows only the steady passing of its daylight and its inevitably approaching dissolution in a darkness that is without dawn. Via the eye, death is made to appear as certain as the arithmetically calculated construction of the verses and the contrived pairing of its features (in the poem's only two eight-syllabic verses, the life of the islands, still visible on the horizon, is tied to the nocturnal voices, only audible when life has departed). Via the ear,

"Meeresstrand" becomes an altogether shattering experience when the accompanying acoustic properties of its cadences flood past the ear into the mainstream of the listener's emotions, like the unabating rhythm of the roaring breakers along the shore.

III *Klaus Groth*

When, in 1894, the eldest daughter of Ferdinand Freiligrath, the illustrious revolutionary poet of March 1848, sought to introduce the German lyric of the nineteenth century to an English-speaking public with a book of translations,[20] she drew more heavily upon Klaus Groth than upon any other lyricist of Poetic Realism. In doing so, of course, she corroborated the generally held opinion of the other anthologists who had been close to the fountainhead of 1848: that Groth's verse constituted a towering pinnacle of creative force in Germany after the middle of the century. But Kate Freiligrath Kroeker (1845–1904), more sensitive—because of her background— to the moods of revolution and literary change than other post-1848 anthologists, went a step further than those who had collected and surveyed German poetry for German audiences; she endeavored to show that Groth had provided the movement of Poetic Realism with the largest number, by far, of its status poems.

This may surprise modern critics who have let Groth drift into the slough of abysmal neglect, but Freiligrath's daughter was not altogether without justification in considering Groth's lyrics to be unusually representative of the art of German post-1848 poetry, for his collection of fifty-eight poems entitled *Quickborn* (Living Fountain), when published in November 1852, had soon made him popular in all Low German lands from the Baltic provinces of eastern Europe to as far west as Holland and Flanders. Julian Schmidt spoke of the book's "triumphal march" through Germany.[21] One expanded edition quickly followed the other. By the end of the century, the volume was in its twenty-fifth edition and contained more than twice as many poems as had the first printing. In addition, these poems found their way into countless anthologies of the day and were also frequently reprinted in many editions of Groth's collected works. There can be no doubt, therefore, that the poems in *Quickborn*— as Storm, too, once noted—had made Groth "a celebrity."[22]

The author of this remarkable trophy of post-1848 verse was— like Storm—born and raised a subject of the Danish Crown. He

was born in 1819 in Heide, a town in the Danish duchy of Holstein.
For more than half his life he remained a citizen of the Danish
monarchy. His ties to the Danish muse were strong, stronger indeed
than were Storm's; for Groth—unlike Storm—had frequently visited
Copenhagen and had close personal ties with many Danish men of
letters, not the least of whom was Hans Christian Andersen. Not
only did he speak and read Danish well, but, as he once acknowledged, he also "thought half in Danish."[23]

It is scarcely surprising that Groth, when he began to write verse,
inherited, like Storm, the musical tradition of Danish poetry. His
early verse exhibits a high degree of fascination with the opera of
emotion. Typical are the following verses of April 1846, in which
subjective feeling and birdlike song merge into a harmonious tune:

> Von deinen Lippen ist der Ton erklungen,
> Der sonnenwärts mein ganzes Wesen zieht,
> Du hast ihn in die Seele mir gesungen,
> Sieh, was ich denke, wird davon ein Lied.[24]

> (Your lips have sent the note of joy a-ringing,
> Which sunward pulls my very being on,
> Into my soul you've led its gladsome singing,
> Behold, my thoughts will now become a song.)

> *Translated by Richard D. Hacken*

But if it can be said that in Groth's pre-1848 "Danish" period the
same sort of romantic musical imagination prevailed that had been
typical of Storm's early verse, then for Groth, too, this world of
comforting melody abruptly crumbled when the fires of 1848 spread
to his native Holstein. The bloodstained soil of that duchy during
its rebellious uprising against the Danish Crown immediately
opened Groth's eyes to harsh reality. Quickly he turned to writing
political poetry in support of the revolution, and—uniquely—he
penned these new verses in the Low German spoken by the rebel
soldiers. One of the first of these poems, written in the spring of
1848, bore the title "Dütsche Ehr un Dütsche Eer" (German Honor
and German Earth). The first stanza reads:

> Dar keemn Soldaten æwer de Elf,
> Hurah, hurah, na't Norn!

Se keemn so dicht as Wagg an Wagg,
Un as en Koppel vull Korn.

(There came soldiers across the Elbe,
Hurrah, hurrah, to the North!
They came as thick as wave on wave,
And like a field full of corn.)

Translated by Max Müller[25]

These are the verses of a war song, of patriotic invective with its
language, rhyme, and rhythm all pressed into the battle for independence from the Danish Crown. With his pen, Groth marched
side by side with the soldiers pushing northward in the spring of
1848 in what seemed—in those early months of the war—to be a
successful fight to drive the Danish occupation forces from his homeland.

The chief characteristic of these verses is that they were written
in the Low German tongue of the insurgents. Set in the spoken
vernacular of the rebels, the verses could more easily win support
for the revolutionary cause. This was a real novelty, for until Groth
started to pen his war lyrics, Low German was hardly considered
a valid medium for poetry. Not since the early sixteenth century,
when Burkard Waldis had put Low German into verse form in
support of the Protestant Reformation, had this form of speech been
used effectively as a poetic idiom. Groth now thought much as
Waldis had 300 years earlier: if people were to be rallied around
the cause he was championing, the verses had to be composed in
the natural, undistorted idiom of the people who read them.
Waldis's mission had been to protest against something in religion,
the burning issue of his day; Groth's concern was the overriding
one in his time and locale: to win converts and kindle enthusiasm
for the uprising against the Crown of Denmark.

Groth was truly innovative in his political poetry, and his sympathy for the duchy's struggle for independence never wavered;
still, he was ill prepared for a vocation limited to writing political
pamphlets in verse. His deep roots in the colorful garden of Danish
song gave him little patience with a narrow branch of poetry that
could not look beyond a current political issue. So he stopped using
his pen in the revolutionary cause and sought, instead, to renew
his interest in the more enduring poetic form of Danish verse-

melody, though without losing sight of the reality to which he had been rudely alerted by the revolution.

It was then that he commenced writing his *Quickborn*. The book is a melodious composition in the Danish sense, a felicitous bouquet of buoyant songs, stirring ballads, and rollicking idylls. But for all its high spirits and harmonious tones, the book is no less a moving diorama of real life; it is graphic proof that Groth could not forget the heat of war, the roar of cannon in the distance, and the armed Danish sentry occasionally standing guard in front of his house.[26] Yet Groth's new poetic presentation of real life is not an illustration of the pitched battles of 1848, as was the political poetry. It seeks to bring the stern tragedy of the human struggle for life to the fore.

On their most obvious level, these poems offer a true picture of the land and people of Groth's native countryside, both present and past. The verses describe, with a considerable breadth and uncanny accuracy, the people Groth knew so well: the homely folk of farmers and fishers, at work and at play. Most importantly, this portrayal preserves a fidelity of language which gives this slice of real life its only possible genuine expression. As was the case with Groth's political poetry, the idiom actually found among the Holstein people—whose feelings and manners Groth depicts—adds a touch of local color that makes *Quickborn* come doubly alive. But Groth did not intend merely to set forth the characteristic features of a local region, as Auerbach and Kompert had done in their prose. He wished, rather, to employ these features as a means of stating commonly perceptible truths of human existence. Very specifically, Groth stated that he wanted to present a "mirror" of real life, a "poetically transfigured" world, in which men could discover themselves.[27]

Groth is at his best in those parts of *Quickborn* that are composed in ballad form. In those parts, real life, real places, and the real language spoken by the folk between the North Sea and the Baltic blend most harmoniously with the poetic melody of the Danish lyre. For balladry is at home in Denmark; Danish ballads are second to those of no other country. It is perhaps not without significance that two militant patrons of the balladry of Denmark, the poet Bernhard Ingemann (1789–1862) and the historian Johannes Steenstrup (1844–1935), made highly successful translations of the *Quickborn* ballads into Danish.[28] Nor is it by chance that, soon after *Quickborn* was published, an influential Danish literary critic, Carl

Rosenberg (1829–1885), spoke of Groth as an "ally" of Danish culture.[29] Hans Christian Andersen, after reading *Quickborn*, sensed a compelling kinship with Groth.[30] And by 1857 even the King of Denmark himself, Frederic VII, felt obliged to offer Groth—notwithstanding the bitterness of the recently quelled revolution—an annuity from the coffers of the Crown.[31]

Of all the *Quickborn* ballads that were so remarkably well attuned to the pulse of Danish melody, and yet so German in their realism, few have attracted as much attention from the critics as has "Ol Büsum" (Old Büsum), composed late in 1851. Storm considered it to be one of the three best poems in the whole of *Quickborn*:[32]

> Ol Büsen liggt int wille Haff,
> De Floth de keem un wöhl en Graff.
>
> De Floth de keem un spöl un spöl,
> Bet se de Insel ünner wöhl.
>
> Dar blev keen Steen, dar blev keen Pahl,
> Dat Water schœl dat all hendal.
>
> Dar weer keen Beest, dar weer keen Hund,
> De ligt nu all in depen Grund.
>
> Un Allens, wat der lev un lach,
> Dat deck de See mit depe Nach.
>
> Mitünner in de holle Ebb
> So süht man vunne Hüs' de Köpp.
>
> Denn dukt de Thorn herut ut Sand,
> As weert en Finger vun en Hand.
>
> Denn hört man sach de Klocken klingn,
> Denn hört man sach de Kanter singn,
>
> Denn geit dat lisen dœr de Luft:
> "Begrabt den Leib in seine Gruft."[33]
>
> (Old Büsum lies 'neath angry wave,
> The waters came and scooped its grave.
>
> The stealthy tide crept sure and slow,
> Till it had gnawed the island through.

No fence remained, nor stick nor stone,
The waves washed all remorseless down.

Nor dog nor beast again gave sound,
They all lie deep on ocean's ground.

And all who lived and laughed in light,
The sea has covered with black night.

Sometimes at lowest ebb you see
The tops of houses in the sea.

A steeple points from out the sand,
As 'twere the finger of a hand.

Then hears one low the church bells ring,
Then hears one low the cantor sing,

Then sounds the hymn below today:
"This body in the grave we lay.")

Translated by Richard D. Hacken

Immediately noticeable in this poem are several characteristics that were popular with the Danish ballad: the basic narrative foundation, the impersonal tone, the bold dramatic outline, the simple two-line stanza with four accentuated syllables in each verse and, of course, the plaintive melody echoing forth from the repetitions of iambs and rhyming couplets. These balladic features combine with the realistic portrayal of the sinking of the island of Büsum in the North Sea, an actual historical event.

The first three stanzas poetically recreate the eroding action of the restless waves and show the island's vulnerability before the raging sea. The fourth and fifth stanzas bemoan the drowning of all living things. Stanzas six and seven speak hauntingly of monuments of man's past habitations protruding through the waves to remind later generations that their predecessors had perished in the watery depths. The church spire, graphically compared to a human finger reaching forth out of the sandy shallows, warns posterity that it, too, will be engulfed in the inescapable floods of death. The final two stanzas appropriately conclude the ballad with mournful death knells from the belfry of the church steeple, and with the eerie chant of a lonely cantor singing the first line of a funeral hymn by the eighteenth-century poet Friedrich Gottlieb Klopstock:

> Begrabt den Leib in seine Gruft.
>
> (This body in the grave we lay.)

Significantly, this last line deliberately omits Klopstock's exultant antiphonal song of conquest over death's sting, for the opening stanza of Klopstock's hymn had the following text:

> Begrabt den Leib in seine Gruft,
> Bis ihm des Richters Stimme ruft!
> Wir säen ihn; einst blüht er auf,
> Und steigt verklärt zu Gott hinauf![34]
>
> (This body in the grave we lay
> There to await that solemn Day!
> When God Himself shall bid it rise
> To mount triumphant to the skies!)

> *Translated by William M. Czamanske*

In Groth's poem this possibility of an afterlife is not raised; nothing remains but the finality of death.

As with Storm's "Meeresstrand," the rich melody of Groth's lines orchestrates the tone of the ballad's narrative and forces the tormenting meditation on the ephemerality of life to linger on in the listener's senses, stirring his emotions. In addition, the sound of the Low German folk-speech lets the somberness of the life-and-death theme penetrate into the ear in the form of a primal cry. The short lines and short stanzas reflect a form of natural lamentation, as if the advancing dread were being interrupted by groaning and sighing. The regular iambic beat echoes the steady rhythm of the tolling funeral bells and lends a forward thrust to the narrative, emphasizing time's quick passing. The combination of forward movement and interruptive pause, the alternation of short and long stresses, and the consistent series of rhymed couplets produce a sense of duality, which serves to underscore the conviction that life is always followed by death. The dramatic manner in which this agonizing realization is unfolded cuts to the core of the listener's soul. Not statically, but in constant confrontation of both image and meter, the interlocked apparitions of life and death are made to meet in furious but hopeless dialogue. Dramatically, moreover, a crescendo of suspense and anxiety overtakes mortal man toward the end of the poem, as the eerie voices from beyond are introduced by the ominously repeated adverb of inexorably moving time: *Denn*.

The abrupt departure from visual imagery in the final two stanzas, where the lines insistently appeal to auditory stimuli (life is no longer visible above the waves), prepares the ear for the funeral service after the completion of life's cycle, for the hymn of death deprived of Klopstock's comforting hope of resurrection.

Life has always been indifferent and fleeting, or so the impersonal tone of the ballad reminds us. It was that way centuries ago before old Büsum was swallowed up by the sea; it is that way now while the foaming sea lurks insidiously beyond the rampart of sandy shallows; and it will remain that way for all generations to come.

IV   *Gottfried Keller*

Storm and Groth had quickly become prophets of the new age in German poetry; the lyricist Keller, on the other hand, took a long time to implant fully in his verse the virtues of Poetic Realism. For almost a quarter of a century after 1848 it looked as though Keller's roots in the German lyric tradition antedating 1848 were contravening the canon of the postrevolutionary age and preventing him from assuming a position of preeminence in the lyric realm. In his heart and mind he naturally sought to capture the spirit of the contemporary movement; his personal experiences in the revolutions compelled him to do so. Yet the style of his poetry well into the 1870s betrays his difficulty in ridding himself of a form of verse that was more at home in romanticism than in the new realism. The delay in Keller's maturing as a representative lyricist of Poetic Realism stands out all the more noticeably, of course, when contrasted with his early achievement in the genre of the novella, where he had succeeded in establishing himself as a paragon of the new creative force very soon after the revolutionary conflagrations.

This delay, unfortunately, has prevented many critics from conceding that Keller is just as deserving of a high ranking in German poetry of the nineteenth century as were, for instance, Storm and Groth. The attitude of the critic Fontane immediately comes to mind. In no edition of his influential anthology *Deutsches Dichter-album* did he see fit to include a single poem by Keller; and even as late as 1894, four years after the poet's death, Fontane remained unwilling to admit that Keller's poetry was particularly distin-guished.[35] It is true, of course, that the shadow of prerevolutionary poetry lingered in the background and that its stifling presence can be detected in all succeeding collections of Keller's verse (to such an extent, in fact, that it could not possibly escape Fontane's dis-cerning eye). But it was not so firmly anchored that Keller could not eventually remove it; and when he finally did succeed in doing so—in certain poems—his poetry acquired the genuine ring of Po-etic Realism so thoroughly and convincingly that there could no longer be any doubt of Keller's distinguished standing amongst the leading lyricists of his age. Fontane and those critics who followed in his footsteps made a blunder in dismissing Keller as a mediocre poet.

Keller's poetry can be divided into three rather distinct phases. The first of these concluded with the publication of his first volume of verse, *Gedichte*, in 1846. The second phase ended with his *Neuere Gedichte*, the first edition of which appeared in 1851 and the second, slightly augmented one in 1854. The climax of Keller's career as a lyricist came with his *Gesammelte Gedichte* of 1883.

Of some 150 poems in Keller's earliest collection, the first of his "Waldlieder" (Woodland Songs) has proved to be the one most frequently reprinted in anthologies of German verse. It is quoted here according to the version which appeared in *Gedichte*; more modern editions have invariably incorporated revisions subse-quently undertaken by Keller, and these no longer truly reflect the temper of his pre-1848 poetry:

> Arm in Arm und Kron' an Krone steht der
>   Eichenwald verschlungen,
> Heut hat er bei guter Laune mir sein altes Lied
>   gesungen.
>
> Fern am Rand fing eine junge Eiche an sich sacht
>   zu wiegen,
> Und dann ging es immer weiter an ein Sausen, an
>   ein Biegen;
>
> Kam es her in mächt'gem Zuge, schwoll es an zu
>   breiten Wogen,

Hoch sich durch die Wipfel wälzend kam die
    Sturmesfluth gezogen.

Und nun sang und pfiff es graulich in den Kronen,
    in den Lüften,
Und dazwischen knarrt' und dröhnt' es unten in
    den Wurzelgrüften.

Manchmal schwang die höchste Eiche gellend
    ihren Schaft alleine:
Donnernder erscholl nur immer drauf der Chor
    vom ganzen Haine!

Einer wilden Meeresbrandung hat das schöne
    Spiel geglichen,
Alles Laub war, weißlich schimmernd, starr nach
    Süden hingestrichen.

Also streicht die alte Geige Pan der Alte, laut und
    leise,
Unterrichtend seine Wälder in der alten
    Weltenweise.

In den sieben Tönen schweift er unerschöpflich auf
    und nieder,
In den sieben alten Tönen, die umfassen alle
    Lieder.

Und es lauschen still die jungen Dichter und die
    jungen Finken,
Kauernd in den dunklen Büschen sie die
    Melodieen trinken.[36]

(Stands the mighty oaken forest, waving leafy
    summits hoary,
And to-day, in high good humour, it has sung its
    old, old story.

First began a tender sapling, gently in the breezes
    bending,
Then the tempest gathered fury, ever growing,
    roaring, rending.

Lo, it sweeps in stormy billows, rolling by in
    solemn gladness;

Raving through the highest branches shrieks the
wind aloud in madness.

High o'erhead now howls the tempest, wildly
whistling, weirdly moaning;
Deep below, amongst the rootwork, you can hear
it creaking, groaning.

Sometimes yells a single oak tree, brandishing its
shaft to heaven,
Thundering answer gives the forest, tumult wild of
leafy leaven.

Even to a boiling springtide this grand pastime all
resembled,
Towards the North the foliage whitened; wind-
swept, silver gray it trembled.

Thus, now playing loud, now softly, doth old Pan
still strike his lyre,
Teaching all his woods and forests his world-
ancient chaunt and quire.

Inexhaustibly he wanders up and down his gamut
sweeping,
That in seven tones containeth the world-harmony
in its keeping.

And 'neath dripping leaves, young poets and young
fledglings cower shrinking,
While in silence they both listen, all the melody
in-drinking.)

Translated by Kate Freiligrath Kroeker[37]

The poem reveals that Keller was an extraordinarily gifted lyricist
from the start. Rarely has an oak forest been recreated as majestically
as in these stately trochaic octameter couplets, and few poets have
succeeded in making it sing as Keller does in these lines. All the
voices of the forest seem to come alive. Theodor Storm and Georg
Scherer were so impressed with the intrinsic beauty of this poem
that both—in their respective anthologies—placed it at the very
beginning of those sections where they sought to win friends for
Keller's poetry.[38] Freiligrath's daughter did the same when she
introduced Keller's verse to the English-speaking world.[39]

Yet for all its rich poetic life, the poem is far from being representative of Poetic Realism. Written in August 1845, well before
the scathing effects of the revolution had touched the poet, its
dominant feature is the artistic surrender to a subjective feeling of
enchantment. The poem's penultimate line makes this at once
graphically evident: poets, like finches in the bushes, are nature's
docile pupils. At the end, the reader comes away with the impression that the poem's scene-painting (admirable painting, to be sure)
occupies so much space that it leaves too little room for the trans-
figuration of reality that was to become the earmark of the poetry
of Poetic Realism. In these verses Keller clearly reveals himself as
being steeped in the prerevolutionary tradition of German nature
song, particularly as it was embodied in the *Gedichte* of the Swiss
nature-lover Johann Gaudenz von Salis-Seewis (1762–1834), published in Keller's own native Zurich in 1816.

If in Keller's most successful prerevolutionary lyrics the elements
of subjective joy, natural beauty, and magical ecstasy are emphasized and their contraries seemingly ignored, if Keller's best poetry
from his earliest period appears, in short, to be romantically escapist, the dominant characteristic of his second lyric phase is a curious
ambivalence which reveals itself in realistic undertones subjacent
to these enchanting worlds. There is a noticeably stronger consciousness of reality in the *Neuere Gedichte*, for Keller put the
finishing touches on them during the summer of 1849 when the
ashes of the revolution in Baden were still smoldering.[40] Nevertheless, this second volume of poems does not constitute a whole-
hearted or successful rejection of romantic escapism. Even though
Keller had been personally caught up in the revolutionary whirlwind
and had witnessed firsthand some of the bloodiest spectacles of the
Badensian revolution, the verse of this volume still gravitates heavily toward the world of fantasy which antedated the horror of revolution. In 1851, when the volume was published, and even as late
as 1854, when the augmented edition appeared, Keller's lyrics were
still not liberated from the tradition of pre-1848 poetry. And it can
be safely assumed that this was the reason why the post-1848 public,
now so closely attuned to the world of revolution, did not take well
to the poems in the volume, which sold badly. Yet, despite the fact
that these poems tend to deal in magical worlds that invariably steer
the reader's imagination away from reality, this new poetry of
Keller's revolutionary period had acquired a certain sense of depth

and realistic substantiality not typical of the best poems in his first volume of verse. Definite progress had been made in Keller's development into a lyricist of Poetic Realism.

The poem "Winternacht" (Winter Night) clearly forms the high-water mark of the *Neuere Gedichte*. Of all the poems in the volume, it is the one most obviously possessing the qualities of artistic greatness. The reception of Keller's *œuvre* has confirmed this opinion again and again.[41] Storm referred to it in 1878 as the first of only three poems by Keller which he would classify as immortal.[42] Leonard Forster has narrowed this down further in judging "Winternacht" to be one of only two outstanding poems composed by Keller.[43] Robert M. Browning, another modern anthologist of German verse, has taken the ultimate step of singling out "Winternacht" as the one and only great specimen of Keller's art of verse-making.[44] Of all Keller's poems, it has proved to be *the* perennial favorite with translators:

> Nicht ein Flügelschlag ging durch die Welt,
> Still und blendend lag der weiße Schnee,
> Nicht ein Wölklein hing am Sternenzelt,
> Keine Welle schlug im starren See.
>
> Aus der Tiefe stieg der Seebaum auf,
> Bis sein Wipfel in dem Eis gefror;
> An den Aesten klomm die Nix' herauf,
> Schaute durch das grüne Eis empor.
>
> Auf dem dünnen Glase stand ich da,
> Das die schwarze Tiefe von mir schied;
> Dicht ich unter meinen Füßen sah
> Ihre weiße Schönheit Glied für Glied.
>
> Mit ersticktem Jammer tastet' sie
> An der harten Decke her und hin.
> Ich vergess' das dunkle Antlitz nie,
> Immer, immer liegt es mir im Sinn![45]

> (Not a wing beat through the frozen air,
> Calm and silent lay the dazzling snow,
> Not a cloud hung on the night-sky fair,
> Not a wave stirred the numb lake below.
>
> From its depth arose the coral-tree

Till its summit touched the ice and froze;
Climbing up upon its branches free,
Gazing upwards still, the Nixie rose.

And I stood upon the fragile glass
Which divided that black gulf from me,
Close, close under foot I saw her pass,
Her white beauty limb by limb did see.

And with stifled moan she gropes along
That hard roof, all green and crystalline;
Never, never shall I cease to long
For that sweet dark face so close to mine!)

Translated by Kate Freiligrath Kroeker[46]

The poem is remarkable on account of its evocation of chilling stillness and absolute futility. The opening stanza depicts the landscape as frozen and strangled by the icy grip of winter. Every vowel is stiffly frozen in the tightly knit trochaic verse scheme; each line of verse not only begins with a harsh, icy vowel sound, but also terminates with the final beat of the last trochee choked off in catalectic fashion. In the central two stanzas, a nymph is described pathetically groping about under the ice that imprisons the lake. This dream creature from the realms of fantasy finds herself blocked at the stringent bounds of reality. She appears as a symbol of life trying in vain to free herself from the freezing clutches of death. The concluding quatrain of the poem commences with the nymph still struggling (now in her final, stifled agony of despair) for some sort of release; it ends as the poet hypnotizes himself with the contemplation of the nymph's now-extinct beauty. Throughout the poem, the heavy, uniformly masculine endings of each line give added stress to the poet's rendition of deep, lingering pain.

The chief advance of "Winternacht" over the first of the "Waldlieder" is the noticeable evolution in Keller's disconcerting realization of the certainty of death, as contrasted to the earlier mood of romantic peace in the majestic solitude of nature. A sense of time and death, so typical of the poetry of German Poetic Realism, has now strikingly begun to show itself.

But if a noticeable shift toward Poetic Realism has been made in this poem, it is still freighted with imagery nonetheless bound by communion with romantic powers. Despite the emerging contemplation of life's verities, the most impressive parts of the poem are those quickening the imagination with mystical rapture. They still serve as vivid testimony to Keller's original baptism in romantic thought; the verses breathe the enchanting magic of winter and the sentimentality of inhibited love. On the whole, the poem conveys the impression of realism eluded. That reality which had surfaced in allusions to time and death disappears all too quickly behind the figure of the ambiguous nymph; the poet yields to the temptation of withdrawing into prerevolutionary rhetoric, glittering imagery, and subjective fantasy. There can be little cause for wonder, therefore, at Keller's statement, made in the summer of 1849, that his *Neuere Gedichte* constituted his "farewell" to lyric poetry.[47] The most exemplary poem in this volume, after all, was not completely in stride with the positive step toward Poetic Realism he wished to take after his harrowing experiences in the Badensian rebellion.

The revolutionary period in Keller's life had come and gone, and for years it seemed as though he would never succeed in freeing himself of the shackles of prerevolutionary verse. By 1857 he had clearly come to the realization that he could no longer continue to write poetry in the former vein, yet he was equally aware that the *tabula rasa* necessary to bring about a new phase of lyric production remained lacking; in order to make the transition he needed, as he felt, at least a quarter of a year of free time.[48] Finally, in the 1870s, the breakthrough came, and Keller wrote new poems thoroughly in tune with Poetic Realism. In those poems from the earlier volumes which seemed too heavily tainted with romantic escapism, he purged many of their pre-1848 strains; and he also completely revised some early lyrics which he had formerly considered too politically contentious for publication—such as a poem addressed to "Revolution" itself—in order to give them poetic significance. The end result of this tremendous flurry of lyric activity was the appearance of Keller's third and largest volume of poetry, his *Gesammelte Gedichte*, in 1883. It turned out to be his most successful adventure in the lyric: within a year, a second printing became necessary.

By far the most celebrated poem in the volume is "Abendlied" (Evensong), which, more than any other, has come to insure Keller's abiding place as a lyricist of Poetic Realism. Only a few days after reading the poem, Storm dispatched a letter to Zurich to congratulate his Swiss friend. Storm called the poem "the purest lyric gold" and went on to say: "I've read it many times, again and again, to myself and to others, and everyone who heard it was touched by it. I extend to you, dearest friend, my sincere congratulations. Such gems are rare. Even the best poets produce only a very few poems of such quality."[49]

It is not too hard to understand why Storm rated this poem so highly, for with it Keller succeeded in submitting his considerable lyrical talent totally to the demands of Poetic Realism. In "Abendlied" the song of time and death, so central to the lyric of the German Poetic Realists, forms the substance of Keller's poem, instead of merely contributing to the atmosphere, as it did in "Winternacht." Gone are all traces of an artistic surrender to the prerevolutionary influence of Salis-Seewis, to romantic escapism, or to anything else that had antedated the great watershed of 1848. At last Keller, the lyricist, had caught up with Storm and Groth:

> Augen, meine lieben Fensterlein,
> Gebt mir schon so lange holden Schein,
> Lasset freundlich Bild um Bild herein:
> Einmal werdet ihr verdunkelt sein!
>
> Fallen einst die müden Lider zu,
> Löscht ihr aus, dann hat die Seele Ruh';
> Tastend streift sie ab die Wanderschuh',
> Legt sich auch in ihre finst're Truh'.
>
> Noch zwei Fünklein sieht sie glimmend steh'n,
> Wie zwei Sternlein, innerlich zu seh'n,
> Bis sie schwanken und dann auch vergeh'n,
> Wie von eines Falters Flügelweh'n.
>
> Doch noch wandl' ich auf dem Abendfeld,
> Nur dem sinkenden Gestirn gesellt;
> Trinkt, o Augen, was die Wimper hält,
> Von dem goldnen Ueberfluß der Welt![50]
>
> (Eyes, ye treasured windows of my sight,
> Have so long allowed me precious light;
> Letting hosts of images delight,
> Ere the fall of nature's darkening night.
>
> When some day your weary lids must close,

Light fades out, the soul can find repose;
Gropingly her shoes aside she throws,
Lays her in her coffin so morose.

Yet two sparks she sees aglow on high,
Like two stars that charm the inner eye,
Till they flicker, and they too must die,
Wafted off on wings of butterfly.

Still I linger on the evening weald,
With the sinking sun to share the field,
Drink, O eyes, all that the lashes shield
Of the golden wealth the world doth yield.)

Translated by D. G. Wright[51]

The first stanza opens under the lurking shadows of a descending eventide, as the title of the poem indicates. Yet, when the first verse is heard, something of the gladdening light of day can still be perceived. The poet's eyes, in the twilight of his life, are still able to admit the wondrous sights of this world. Hence, the poet has cause to remain delightfully and serenely happy. S. S. Prawer has masterfully shown how this blissful satisfaction echoes through the beginning verses as far as the disruptive colon of the third line: the caressing words *lieb, hold,* and *freundlich* constitute major points of emphasis in the stanza, and these are reinforced by the endearing diminutive *Fensterlein,* by the numerous liquid consonants, and by the constant rhyme on *ei,* associated with *Schein,* with light.[52] Clearly, the joy of daylight has not yet departed. But life's brief day is inexorably waning; after the extended pause at the end of the third line, the heavy-sounding *u* of *verdunkelt* alerts us to the gathering darkness of nightfall.

The second stanza intensifies the feeling of life ebbing away. The gloomy *u* of *verdunkelt* becomes the rhyming vowel and dominant sound of the entire stanza, lingering on at the end of each line. The cheerful light of *Schein* in the first stanza has now been supplanted by the foreboding doom of *verdunkelt.* We observe, too, a weary human being with the failing faculties of old age—as the uncertain groping associated with the word *tastend* suggests—approaching his appointed end. He lays aside his traveling boots, for he has completed his journey through life's daytime and is ready for the inevitable repose which follows within the dark confines of either the coffin or the grave (*finst're Truh'*, the stanza's final image, could mean either of these things, and probably means both).

The third stanza begins with an image of the final moments of the poet's departing life-light, before the falling shroud of darkness completely extinguishes it. The eyes, which for so long have been the windows of his soul, appear to the dying poet, now that his hours of life have run out, as two faintly flickering candle-flames on the verge of extinction. Prawer's classic analysis of this poem shows how the final departure from this life is musically transmitted to the ears of the listeners: in the third stanza's concluding two lines, the stresses, which hitherto had been so heavy, become less marked (as though a heart were ceasing to beat!), and the last signs of life in the stanza fade away with the whispering sounds of the consonants f, w, s, and l:[53]

> Wie von eines Falters Flügelweh'n.
>
> (Wafted off on wings of butterfly.)

In the barely audible sound of the last dying breath of -*weh'n* (wafting away), musically linked by rhyme to *vergeh'n* (passing away), life has expired.

Much in Keller's "Abendlied" to this point discloses its remarkable affinity to Storm's "Meeresstrand." Here again we witness a poetic interplay of musical sound and realistic portrayal in the form of a *Lied*; again we hear a melody evoking a meditation on the ephemerality of human life. With vigorous pictorial imagery Keller reminds us—as had Storm—of the ebbing of life, of falling eventide at the end of man's day on earth, of the ever-deepening darkness, of the dimming of earth's joys (in this instance, the gradual closing of the eyes), and, of course, of the final snuffing out of life. Moreover, the orchestral accompaniment of vowels, consonants, rhymes, and stresses—similar to those of Storm—allows this song of transiency to flow effortlessly into the ear and profoundly affect the listener's feelings. The certainty of life's passing is acoustically echoed in this poem, furthermore, by the regular, unwavering beat of the slow and measured trochaic verse, much as it had been in Storm's poem by the plangent rhythm of waves breaking interminably along the shore.

But if, in the first three stanzas, Keller's song of time and death seems to have much in common with Storm's song (and to a certain extent also with Groth's), the fourth stanza radically differs from it, as its first line quickly makes apparent. The sudden change in musical effect immediately jolts the listener: instead of continuing the unerring trochaic beat, which had been so regular up to now that it almost lulled the reader to sleep, the first three words of this verse now suddenly all hold stresses, as Prawer's fine musical analysis has so aptly shown:[54]

> Doch noch wandl' ich auf dem Abendfeld
> (–   –   –   ˘   –   ˘   –   ˘   –)
> (Still I linger on the evening weald)

The word *noch* receives a stress to which it is not entitled according to the poem's otherwise stringently regular trochaic pentameter. That makes it—and this line—stand out musically from the rest of the poem. Thus, despite the fast-falling eventide of his life, the poet emphatically states that he is *still* walking the pathway of life and is *still* very much alive. The poet uses image as well as meter to turn the clock back from the final dissolution. As if the musical insistence upon living were not enough, he also paints an exuberant picture of the munificence he enjoys, of the last golden rays in which he is walking. The line's last word, *Abendfeld,* is a word coined by Keller in order to unite both time and place in one image; it suggests, at once, the eventide of life and the rich state of the fields in autumn, when the grain is at its fullest, ripest, and most plentiful. The rest of the stanza depicts the setting sun flooding the horizon with light and radiating "golden superabundance"; at the end, we have a heavy, lingering stress on *Welt.* Everything in this stanza, therefore, contrives to record a genial affirmation of life and to set a counterpoint to the mood of the first three stanzas. Death's triumphant surety links with a magnificent celebration of life.

Implicit in Keller's song is an understanding of the reality of time and decay, certainly, but one which recognizes joy as an essential attribute of living, even though death impends. It knows nothing of that crueler dualism that sees human life as a gloom to be consummated miserably in death. Transiency and death are neither overlooked nor embraced; they stand forth just as sharply as they did in the songs of Storm and Groth, but this time the counterweight of tellurian delights soothes the sting of inevitable death. Yet, this poem is not escapist. It is a poem not of flight, but of courage to insist on the affirmation of a life that is precarious and fleeting. The skill of an experienced poetic craftsman has been applied to a vision that is as realistic as it is serene.

V Conrad Ferdinand Meyer

Conrad Ferdinand Meyer was the last, yet not least luminous, of the bright stars in the galaxy of great lyricists of German Poetic Realism. The definitive collection of his verse, *Gedichte,* actually appeared one year before Keller's *Gesammelte Gedichte,* in 1882, and if this publication date were the sole criterion for establishing priorities, then Meyer would have to precede Keller in any treatment of their lyrics. But Keller, it must be remembered, had been an early convert to Poetic Realism, whereas Meyer was a latecomer. The fact that Keller's post-1848 lyrics spring from the same source as do his novellas puts much of his poetry chronologically ahead of Meyer's. The seeds for Keller's realistic lyrics had been sown early; they took a long while to grow only because the soil for his new poetry had been so thickly covered with the brambles of his pre-1848 verse.

In Meyer's case, however, the revolutionary fires of 1848 had been cold for more than a decade when he began to write serious poetry, and almost another decade had to pass before he began to be taken seriously as a poet. Not until 1867 did a publisher venture to print a slender volume of verse using the name of Conrad Ferdinand Meyer as its author (an earlier volume of 1864 had appeared anonymously and had resulted in financial disaster for the publisher). It was anything but early in the movement, therefore, when Meyer awakened to a consciousness of his lyric gifts. This late ripening distinguishes him from Storm, Groth, and Keller, all of whom had been so close to the fountainhead of 1848. One basic difference lies in the fact that Meyer chose and shaped so many of the themes in his poetry from the pages of history. His adherence to this tendency, typical for the latter part of the movement, sets him apart from the earlier initiates of the laureate fraternity within German Poetic Realism. Noticeable, too, is a far weaker fidelity to tonal effect. Storm's "Meeresstrand," Groth's "Ol Büsum," and Keller's "Abendlied" are all essentially *Lieder,* songs crafted—above all—

with a view toward lavish auditory stimuli. Not so with Meyer, in whose poetry the visual element is dominant, while the acoustic properties play a distinctly minor role.

Storm, whose verse displays the strongest penchant for the pulsating rhythms of musical coloration among the German Poetic Realists, was the first to notice the recession of tonal effect in Meyer's poetry. Keller had written to Storm just as the publication of Meyer's *Gedichte* seemed to be imminent, saying that Meyer's volume would be "with regard to form, probably the loveliest book of poems that has appeared for decades."[55] As soon as he had an opportunity to look into Meyer's *Gedichte*, Storm found himself in general agreement with Keller's high praise; but he also had one important reservation to make: "If you were of the opinion earlier," he wrote to Keller, "that the volume would be one of the loveliest books of songs as regards its form, you probably think otherwise, now that it has appeared: he is not a lyric poet; he lacks the direct and powerful expression of feeling which he would need to become one—or perhaps he even lacks the very feeling itself."[56] Storm had mistakenly believed that Keller had referred to Meyer's volume as a *Liederbuch* (book of songs), whereas Keller had actually spoken of a *Gedichtbuch* (book of poems). Since Storm had misunderstood Keller in this matter, he was expecting to see a book of songs. Naturally, he felt a sense of disappointment when the volume finally arrived, for precisely what he found wanting in Meyer's poetry was the pervasive, spontaneous fluency of the songwriter. Still, Storm had to concede that these poems were not totally devoid of the emotional aspect, either; however, the latter was clearly subordinated to the poetic content: "It first has to work its way through the content; but then it often emerges surprisingly."[57]

The clear-cut differences between Meyer and the other leading lyricists of German Poetic Realism understandably abet those who would disassociate Meyer's poetry from the movement. There has been agitation, for instance, aimed at isolating Meyer in his own historical category of verse. "Conrad Ferdinand Meyer stands strangely alone in his time. He belongs to no school or movement of his day," one modern anthologist has said.[58] For others, the lyricist Meyer has become the initiator of a subsequent movement in German literature known as Symbolism. This thesis has been argued particularly doggedly by Heinrich Henel: "My main purpose [for writing a book about Meyer's poetry] is to establish Conrad

Ferdinand Meyer's role as pioneer of the symbolist manner in German verse. . . . Meyer was the first of German symbolists."[59] But Meyer's poetic world, Werner Oberle has rightly replied, is far too strongly oriented toward reality to be connected with the sort of mystical aestheticism that typified the poetry, for example, of a prominent German symbolist like Rainer Maria Rilke (1875–1926).[60] It is certainly true that Meyer's poetry contains no trace of his personal preoccupation with current affairs, his strong support of the newly united German nation, of Bismarck, and of Emperor William II.[61] But this absence of poetic reference to the political world around him still does not offer, as Henel contends, "proof that he was not a realist."[62] For in none of the great poems of German Poetic Realism (of Storm, of Groth, of Keller) is reality crudely equated with the political issues of the day. Indeed, it has come to be one of the distinguishing features of the lyric of German Poetic Realism that the reality depicted—faithful to the precepts of Julian Schmidt—is of a timeless and universal nature. In this regard, Meyer's poetry shows absolute consistency with the lyric of Poetic Realism.

To Julian Schmidt must go the abiding credit for having identified precisely the rightful place of Meyer's lyrics within the movement of Poetic Realism. Modern critics of Meyer's poetry have blithely overlooked the seminal essay, published in 1884 in the *Preußische Jahrbücher*, in which Schmidt addressed himself to Meyer's lyrics.[63] Such oversight is unfortunate, for in this journal the ever-watchful shepherd of German Poetic Realism takes pains to point out the strong ties that securely bind Meyer's lyrics to the movement. Again and again he refers to Meyer's verse as *Lieder*, thereby underscoring one essential point they have in common with the epoch-making lyrics of predecessors like Storm, Groth, and Keller. But Schmidt also clearly recognizes that Meyer's songs differ from earlier ones. Formerly, he says, poets used "melody" as their point of departure, and only afterwards did they select a suitable "content" to blend with the melody. That, at any rate, was the practice in German poetry prior to the advent of Poetic Realism. The last forty years, however, reversed the procedure. With the more recent lyricists the "image" or the "idea" comes first, and then a "melody" is found to adapt to it. This strong predominance of image over melody is, for Schmidt, typical of Meyer's poetry. The statement also corroborates Storm's opinion, even though Schmidt could not have

known what Storm had written in a personal letter to Keller. Both
Schmidt and Storm came to understand, therefore, that Meyer's
lyrics exhibit a genuine blending of realistic imagery and poetic
melody, and both sensed, as well, that in Meyer's particular blending process it was the image, above all, which was most relevant.
Meyer's realistic color, Schmidt goes on to say, displays the background of his native Swiss Alps, the recollections of travel in Italy,
and, of course, reality culled from books of the historic past. But
the "real object" of Meyer's lyrics, Schmidt insists, is the portrayal
of "archetypal human life." Meyer directly conveys life itself, via
the melody, to the reader's heart.

Perusing this essay by the father of German Poetic Realism, one
quickly gathers that for him Meyer would appear to be the most
representative lyricist of his age. Now the ultimate in what should
be accomplished in verse form—to Schmidt's way of thinking—has
finally been achieved. In Meyer's poetry a vital sense of realism
reigns supreme, but this realism is enhanced by a melody which,
though never clouding the imagery with too profuse a symphony
of sound, possesses enough musical force to transfigure the realistic
picture into a candid commentary on a timeless aspect of human
life.

The critic Fontane, it is interesting to note, held a differing opinion. For him, Meyer's lyrics simply lacked beauty and grace,[64]
presumably because their realistic imagery was more compelling
than their tonal beauty. To Fontane the more balanced combination
of hypnotic rhythm and trenchant realism seems to have become
irresistible from the moment he first heard the postrevolutionary
verses of Storm.

It would be fruitless to try to argue which one of these two
outstanding critics erred in over- or underestimating Meyer's
achievement in the lyric. Readers may prefer Storm's *Gedichte* of
1852 with Fontane or Meyer's *Gedichte* of 1882 with Schmidt; but
the essential difference between the two lyric voices remains none
other than that between early and late German Poetic Realism.
Soon after 1848 the new, dramatic emphasis upon reality in the
lyric could move the reader most forcefully when combined with
vestiges of prerevolutionary verse: with a luscious plangency of tonal
effect. Thirty years later, attention could effectively be drawn to
reality without overtly resorting to the auditory appeal.

The crowning jewel of Meyer's poetry is unquestionably "Der

römische Brunnen" (The Roman Fountain). Heinrich Henel, with his sovereign command of the secondary literature about Meyer's poetry, reminds us that this poem has been almost interpreted to death,[65] and that is surely the best proof of its enduring fame:

> Aufsteigt der Strahl und fallend gießt
> Er voll der Marmorschale Rund,
> Die, sich verschleiernd, überfließt
> In einer zweiten Schale Grund;
> Die zweite giebt, sie wird zu reich,
> Der dritten wallend ihre Flut,
> Und jede nimmt und giebt zugleich
> Und strömt und ruht.[66]

> (Up spurts the stream and falling pours
> Its flood into the marble urn,
> Which, veiled in lacy froth, outpours
> Into a second bowl in turn;
> The second swells, it passes on
> Into a third its seething crest,
> And all receive and give as one
> And flow and rest.)

Translated by C. A. Bernd

On the biographical level, the poem constitutes a plastic recollection of a visit by Meyer in 1858 to the Borghese gardens in Rome. There, in the lower part of the gardens, he saw a fountain which made a profound impression upon him. It was a simple, rather austere structure of three weathered marble basins. The waters falling from one basin into another filled the air of the quiet gardens with continuous splashing sounds. Meyer's faithful sister Betsy informs us that her brother became so intrigued with this fountain that on one of the last evenings before he left Rome he returned to the gardens and sought there to preserve his impressions in the form of a poem.[67] Interesting as these facts are, however, they only give us the factual background to the verses. For in the course of almost a quarter of a century Meyer altered and revised this poem many times until—in the final version of 1882, when the memory of the actual visit to Rome had long since faded—the poem became completely transfigured into another vision of reality. The fountain in the Eternal City found itself transformed into the eternal song

of human transience: as incessant as the flow of water from basin
to basin, from beginning to end, so too is the current of life itself
from cradle to coffin, from womb to tomb. This poetically transfigured picture of reality places Meyer's poem squarely in the lyric
tradition of Storm, Groth, and Keller, for in every one of the moving
examples of verse we have discussed, it was precisely the same
spectacle of human transience which rendered the verses mean-
ingful.

Aufsteigt der Strahl gives the poem a lively start; the heavily
intonated first two syllables, deviating from the normal iambic pattern, portray the energetic gushing forth of new life like the spout
of water when it bursts forth from the fountain. Immediately coupled with the rising up of life, however, is the decline which follows
when the water falls again in the antithetical declivity of the second
half of the first line. Just as water must obey the irreversible law
of gravity, so the human being remains subject to the irrevocable
law of life's decline toward death. After the first line, a great reg-
ularity of iambs sets in, and life can be seen to trickle steadily down
to the grave, passing through the three main stages of youth, middle
age, and old age (as the three basins indicate) on its quick journey.
Life finally comes to its appointed end in the last word, *ruht*, that
long, deep-voweled, and heavily accented finale indicating the
everlasting sleep of death.

Between each of life's important stages a short pause intervenes.
Thus, after the forward movement indicative of life has flowed
quickly on from line one into line two by means of the enjambement,
it halts for a brief moment at the end of line two, meeting the
resistance of both the heavy vowel in *Rund* and the comma. Lines
three and four follow a similar pattern: life flows quickly past in a
stream of aquatic *ch, sch,* and *s* sounds, at times trying to halt (as
at the commas in line three), but never able to tarry for long on its
way downstream. The lengthiest pause comes at the end of line
four, as if the retard induced by the semicolon were giving the
second, larger basin more time to fill up, as if middle age were
shown extending over a greater period than that of youth. But again,
the pause does not last. Life pushes inexorably onward and downward into the decline of old age represented by the third and final
basin. Commas in the fifth and sixth lines temporarily act as brakes
upon the tempo, but they never succeed for long. A haunting sum-
marization in the penultimate line informs us that life is nothing

but a succession of comings and goings. Now we are prepared for
the end. As life expires, the quick, rippling flux of iambs draws to
a halt and is replaced by the slow choking sounds of four spasmodic
breaths:

Und strömt und ruht.

$(- \quad - \quad - \quad -)$

(And flow and rest.)

The choking of death shrouds itself, at the same time, in a stream
of mournful *u* sounds which naturally terminate in the last *ruht*, in
the everlasting sleep of death.

Once more, the spectacle of human transience has been presented
to us. Into these verses—as into those of "Meeresstrand," "Ol
Büsum," and "Abendlied"—have been infused the realities of time
and death. And again, there is nothing inexact or nebulous about
them. We see no enchanted pool of a romantic wonderland, only
the clear and very real flow of life moving ever onward toward sure
and certain death. The transfigured subject matter of "Der römische
Brunnen" thus essentially duplicates that of those three poems by
Storm, Groth, and Keller. But the poetic effects differ. Meyer's
poem about time and death is sustained neither by an opulence of
musical sound nor by a rich imagery aglow with color. Everything
takes on a spare and pithy appearance; all descriptive adjectives are
conspicuously absent, as are all references to the surrounding gardens, the verdant foliage, the azure Roman sky, or the glow of the
hot Italian sun. No gradations of light or shade can be perceived.
The terse eight lines seem as compressed as life is short. The vision
of reality finds itself cloaked in a poetic mantle, therefore, which
stifles all emotion. Only feelings of dampness, austerity, and chill
prevail, like the cold, solid marble of the Roman fountain dampened
by the constant trickling of water upon it. The melodious songs of
sorrow at the passing of life ("Meeresstrand," "Ol Büsum") or of joy
in spite of it ("Abendlied") have now been displaced by the bold
contours of a cold architectonic music.[68] What Storm, Groth, and
Keller orchestrated with warm, pulsating melody, Meyer transposes
to a composition of plain and rigid architecture, a structure of cold,
solid marble hewn into an austerely sculptured stanza with a frozen
combination of hardened nouns, verbs, sharp commas, and the
barest minimum of warmth, color, and tune. The rigidity and fri-

gidity of Meyer's architectonic music give him the advantage of being able to face poetically the realness of ephemerality with cooler, more dampened emotions, indeed, even with a conscious feeling of cold indifference to what is, after all, inevitable. With unassailable candor he recognizes the predetermined form of a life ending in the chill of death, and unflinchingly—with neither joy nor sorrow—he acquiesces to it.

CHAPTER 4

The Novel

WHILE Poetic Realism flourished in Germany, across the Channel, in England, the dominant genre of literature was the novel. This has long been recognized. If any lingering doubts remained, these have been dispelled by Geoffrey Tillotson, who reminds us that it is by no means accidental that most of the recent books on nineteenth-century English literature address themselves to the novel.[1] An essentially identical verdict can be pronounced with regard to Germany's more immediate neighbors to the East and West: Russian and French literature of a century ago also achieved its greatest success with the novel. In Spain, at the time, the novel—that literary vehicle by which earlier Hispanic writers had made a striking contribution to world literature—experienced a spectacular revival after having lain dormant for more than two centuries.

Across the map of Europe, then, there was a general flowering of the novel. But neither Germany nor its close neighbor to the north, Denmark, shared in it. On the contrary, in German Poetic Realism, as in mid-nineteenth-century Danish literature, the novel occupied a weak and unenviable position. Beyond the frontiers of Germany and Scandinavia, for instance, the reputation of the novel of German Poetic Realism was trounced with a rigor hardly paralleled in literary history. The English critic George Henry Lewes (1817–1878) unequivocally stated in 1858 that "the novels in Germany are singularly inferior to those of France or England."[2] In France, a writer of no lesser stature than Edmond de Goncourt (1822–1896) recorded in his *Journal* in 1871 that the Germans, at the moment, possessed no novel.[3] In the United States, William Dean Howells (1837–1920) boldly asserted: "I can think of many German novelle that I should like to read again, but scarcely one German novel."[4]

Clearly, the state of the German novel during the age of Poetic

Realism was not a happy one. The novella, as both Lewes and Howells believed, had superseded it as the far more successful form of fiction. Still, the German novel did not go completely to seed. Despite the adverse criticism leveled against it, particularly from abroad, German Poetic Realism did produce an occasional novel of merit. Just as the works of Meïr Goldschmidt (1819–1887) stand out as lonely, but noteworthy, exceptions to the palpable weakness of the Danish novel at the time, so in Germany there are a few significant exceptions to the general rule that Poetic Realism scored triumphs in the novella at the expense of the novel; and any discussion of the movement would remain incomplete if no reference were made to them.

I   Otto Ludwig

Zwischen Himmel und Erde (Between Heaven and Earth) by Otto Ludwig (1813–1865) was the first novel to secure for itself a lasting place in German Poetic Realism. Written in the summer and autumn of 1855 and published in the spring of 1856, it proved an immediate success. A second edition had to be printed two years later; it was followed in turn by further editions. By 1881 the novel was already in its fifth printing. Within an unusually short time it was ranked among the foremost works of the age. One of the influential literary historians in nineteenth-century France, René-Gaspard-Ernest Saint-René Taillandier (1817–1879), lost no time in hailing Ludwig's novel as a landmark in the school of German literature which had emerged under the critical auspices of Julian Schmidt. This review appeared in the widely read *Revue des Deux Mondes* only a few months after the novel had reached France.[5] Schmidt's brother-in-arms, the German writer Gustav Freytag, also hastened to issue a statement calling Ludwig one of the most talented representatives of the new school of realists in German literature.[6] The most triumphant pronouncement of all came, however, when Schmidt himself stepped forth to acclaim the novel as "a work of the first magnitude, one of those few from our century which can be predicted with some assurance to outlive our own generation."[7]

Like so many of the German Poetic Realists, Otto Ludwig had been profoundly stirred by the revolutions of 1848. He had experienced them while living in the Kingdom of Saxony. Early in March 1848 the flurry of revolutionary agitation had spread to this part of

Germany, and unrest and uproar rapidly encompassed the entire kingdom. Leipzig, the largest city in Saxony, was placed under military occupation. Ludwig, closely observing the happenings, wrote at the time to a friend that 8,000 soldiers were encamped around Leipzig, and as a result food was scarce and prohibitively expensive. In the capital city of Dresden, he went on to say, one riot followed the other. For the economy of the country, as well as for the welfare of its population, Ludwig also noted, the revolution was no less than catastrophic. Industry and commerce had become paralyzed; everywhere men were out of work; and starvation ran rampant.[8] This horrible state of affairs continued for more than a year. On May 3, 1849, the citizens of Dresden, in a last desperate effort to bring about a change, tried to take the government arsenal by storm, whereupon royalist troops fired into their midst and into the barricades set up all over the city. The king, fearful of the mob violence, had to flee. Anarchy erupted and blood flowed freely in the streets. Peace came only later in the month when Prussian troops marched into the unhappy kingdom and ruthlessly quelled every last vestige of the rebellion.

For Ludwig, the revolutionary outbursts he had witnessed proved to be a cause of deep concern over the function of literature. He wrote in May of that year that the escapist sort of *belles-lettres* which had been in vogue prior to 1848 was now completely out of fashion and would not easily be revived; but the other type of literature, which had rejected the conventions of pure fancy and had preferred, instead, to support political issues, hardly seemed an alternative to which he could turn. "For every flake of gold which political literature contained," he whimsically said, "there were ten barrow-loads of gravel and mud covering it."[9] Clearly, he realized, an altogether new movement in literature seemed called for.[10]

It was around this time that the writings of Julian Schmidt began to exert a compelling influence over him. They offered him precisely the alternative for which he was looking, and he became wholly absorbed in them. As time went on, he even came into close personal contact with Schmidt, who was also living in Saxony. The two men met to discuss the place of literature in a world still reeling from the aftershocks of insurrection. When they could not meet in person, they corresponded with one another at length. And as if this were not enough, Ludwig also began to enter into an imaginary dialogue with Schmidt. In a letter to the chief architect of German

Poetic Realism, Ludwig wrote that he was filling a notebook with analyses of literature, and that pages and pages of these were written in the form of imaginary letters to his great friend.[11] Under the titanic shadow of Schmidt, Ludwig went on to fill many a notebook with probing inquiries into the nature of literature. Schmidt, it seems, increasingly became Ludwig's figurative conversational partner. Again and again these notebooks give the impression that the apostle of German Poetic Realism is sitting across the room while Ludwig writes, and that the latter is speaking extemporaneously, as if in leisurely conversation with his imaginary partner.[12] These fanciful conversations with Schmidt, as well as the actual ones in oral and written form, became the two springs from which Ludwig now drew heavily. As a devoted disciple of Schmidt, he began to move ever more securely within the orbit of Poetic Realism, for the bulk of these real and imagined conversations focused attention upon Schmidt's antipodal principle of a literature remaining true to actual life and yet operating within a poetic realm. Reality and fantasy: these constituted the twin pillars upon which, according to Ludwig's thinking, a work of literature should be built. The marriage of the two creates, as he stated, "a world that stands midway between the objective truth of things and the law which our [i.e., the poet's] mind is impelled to read into them."[13]

In his constant dialogue with Schmidt, Ludwig was, of course, only reiterating and confirming what German Poetic Realism's missionary founder had been preaching all along, but Ludwig performed his task with such zeal, and even genius, that he soon became something of a second apostle to the movement. In a host of imaginary conversations he worked hard, for instance, to extend the dogma of Poetic Realism to the drama of Shakespeare. Speaking of the latter, he said: "By and large there is no writer who remains so faithful to the truth of life, and yet his details put him thoroughly into the realm of fantasy. . . ."[14]

More ingenious was the discovery, in later phantom dialogues with Schmidt, of the magic formula used to designate everything the father of German Poetic Realism had stood for. Curiously, the movement's originator had never come up with a name for what he had sought to establish. Tirelessly, Schmidt had campaigned for an indissoluble marriage between the two opposing poles of reality and fiction, but it required the ingenuity of his zealous disciple Ludwig to give this literary union its felicitous name *Poetischer Realismus*.[15]

In devising this formula, Ludwig not only lent a new precision to the antipodal principle upon which Schmidt's apostolate firmly rested, but became enormously popular as well. Now, finally, men of letters in Germany could refer to the new literary creed with a label that was ingeniously concise.

Ludwig became so famous for his invention that a tendency developed to think of him, and not Schmidt, as the theoretical father of the new literary movement.[16] This, in turn, provoked a contrary trend of underrating Ludwig's formula. The German philosopher Friedrich Wilhelm Joseph Schelling (1775–1854), it was claimed, had invented the term long before Ludwig.[17] Scholars who continued to believe that the formula had been Ludwig's invention were ridiculed. More recently, however, René Wellek has shown that the term employed by Schelling had nothing whatsoever to do with the paradoxically dichotomous principle governing much of German literature after the middle of the nineteenth century.[18] The credit for coining the formula specifically designed to characterize that literary movement, therefore, should return to Ludwig.

No major author of Poetic Realism became as thoroughly self-educated in the literary creed of Julian Schmidt as did Ludwig. Thinking and writing so extensively under the patronizing influence of Schmidt—so much so that he could even define the concept of *Poetischer Realismus* more precisely and concisely than its founding father—Ludwig naturally became a prime figure in the movement.

In this zealous disciple, the movement's great prophet saw his teachings confirmed, augmented, and splendidly worded. "I was absolutely amazed," Schmidt said, "at how perfectly we agreed in our judgments. But how exquisitely he can express his judgment!"[19] If Ludwig had acquired an astonishing maturity in literary acuity and a superb gift of expression as a result of the real and phantom conversations he carried on with Schmidt, he still never failed to acknowledge that it was the latter who had opened up his eyes and shown him the way. Typical is the following comment: "It was not until I read the dedication in J. Schmidt's book on Schiller [Schmidt had prefaced the volume with a moving tribute to Ludwig] that I had the courage to see, for the first time, what had been right in front of my eyes for so long."[20]

The finest literary fruit that ripened in the course of Ludwig's long and fertile preoccupation with Schmidt's theory of literature is the autobiographical novel *Zwischen Himmel und Erde*. In a brief but important critical statement about the story, Ludwig himself tells us what he sought to portray in the main body of the narrative. The story's central figure, Apollonius—Ludwig says—turned the fear of overtaxing his overly tender conscience into a passion which beclouded his intelligence. Ludwig goes on to say that he intended to portray the typical fate of a man who had too much conscience. That shows up in the contrast delineated between him and his brother, Fritz, who was to illustrate the destiny of a man who had too little conscience. Then the reciprocal effect sets in, as the one burdened with too much conscience forces the other to worsen, and the latter makes the former more and more timorous. The predictable fate of the overconscientious person reveals itself: he gets a headache, so to speak, from what others drink.[21] So much for the central portion of the narrative, as summed up succinctly by Ludwig himself. He presents us with an inescapable reality of life: the necessity to choose between right and wrong, virtue and vice; and he clearly indicates, furthermore, what consequences are felt when these two opposites clash, especially within the same family.

The unusual thing about the novel, however, is that this very genuine concern for ultimate values in everyday life does not unfold simply and straightforwardly, as Ludwig's summary would perhaps lead us to believe. It is not the natural development of the two real passions, nor the obvious contrast between the characters, which makes this novel so remarkable, but rather the fact that this portrayal of human life has been clothed in the fictional garb of reminiscence. The narrator begins, capriciously enough, by boldly telling the end of the story first. The fabric of the novel's realism, therefore, is woven by the cult of memory, which fictionalizes and spiritualizes that reality from a different point in time—some thirty years later—and thereby lifts it out of the realm of real time (there is no note of the story's actual dates and geographic location). Living in peaceful retirement in his advanced years, Apollonius recollects scenes from the drama that had occurred a generation earlier between him and his brother. On the retina of his memory he eagerly retraces certain happenings from his youth, while deliberately forgetting others. The reality of the past, in other words, has been remolded in retrospect and assumes a new, fanciful appearance. Different from before—colored, partial, and biased—the new, remembered experience necessarily distorts and falsifies the original facts. From the autobiographical viewpoint, Apollonius appears more like a saint

than an actual human being. George Henry Lewes, more than a
century ago, keenly detected this falsity (although without realizing
that it was artistically purposeful).[22]

It follows that the overriding conflict which gives this novel its
structure and meaning is neither that of the two brothers nor that
of virtue and vice—as has been frequently claimed—but rather the
fictionally superimposed conflict between an actual, experienced
reality and its subsequent autobiographical transformation in an
imaginative memory unaffected by the laws of true chronology. Fact
and fiction, reality and imagination become the dominant focal
points of interest in the novel; and the reader, once he realizes this,
promptly finds himself confronted with the crucial question: which
is the world of reality and which the world of imagination? On one
level of the narrative, it would seem that the world of the actual
past represents fact, whereas the spell of recollection, which projects
that historical past in a reordered, distorted, and falsified fashion,
comprises the sphere of imagination. On another level of the narrative, however, it could be said that the territory of memory, which
gives a new lease on life to certain past events, is the only real
world presented to us in this novel, while the ordinary sequence
of actual events prior to the memory-recall must be imagined.

The novel may, therefore, be regarded as a fictional statement
about the fundamental roles of fact and imagination in human life.
The narrator of the feigned reality in this novel appears to be struggling as much with these two opposing spheres as did Ludwig himself when, in his theoretical exercises, he pondered the dualistic
structure of Poetic Realism. The aptly named novel *Zwischen Himmel und Erde* thus echoes the same profound concern with the
enigma of reality and imagination that had been characteristic of the
real and imaginary conversations which Ludwig had carried on with
Julian Schmidt.

II   *Wilhelm Raabe*

The second of the particularly noteworthy novels of German Poetic Realism is *Die Chronik der Sperlingsgasse* (The Chronicle of
Sparrow Lane) by Wilhelm Raabe (1831–1910). The author began
writing it in the late autumn of 1854 and completed his work during
the following summer. The novel appeared in October 1856, and
a second edition came out in 1858. Rapidly it became a bestseller

in Germany; by 1910, when the author died, it was already in its seventieth printing. This work headed a long train of ambitious novels that Raabe was to write. Its success encouraged him to write more novels, which added further luster to his name. When the obituaries of Raabe were finally written, however, it became clear that it was his first book, *Die Chronik der Sperlingsgasse*, which had given him the popularity he retained to the end.[23] Even today, more than half a century after Raabe's death and well over a century after its conception, this novel from his youth has lost nothing of its original brilliance. In 1961 Barker Fairley, a leading Raabe critic, confidently said of the novel: "A good case could be made for ranking it with Raabe's best."[24]

As with Ludwig's novel, so *Die Chronik der Sperlingsgasse* moves briskly within the literary stream that started to flow in 1848. Committed to paper only a little more than five years after the revolutions had been quelled, it issued forth from the revolutionary spirit and derived its basic energy from the still-smoldering aftereffects.

When Raabe arrived in Berlin in the spring of 1854, only half a year before he started to write the novel, tangible reminders of the catastrophic events of 1848 were still everywhere in evidence: the economy had been disrupted, food was scarce, prices were high, and unemployment was rampant. The destruction wrought by the revolutions had to be paid for; taxes had become oppressive, bankruptcies an everyday occurrence. Memories of the terror on the streets of Berlin—of the bloody engagements, of the wounded and the dead—were still very much on everyone's mind and lips. Everywhere could be seen bedraggled and hungry people. A pall of defeat, frustration, and despair hung over the entire city, indeed over the whole of Germany. The newspapers gave daily notice of the sad exodus of hapless Germans departing for greener pastures in the United States, the southern provinces of Brazil, and even the coastal regions of Algeria. Hundreds of thousands were hurrying to flee, determined to escape the poverty brought on by political instability. Beginning with 1848, emigration from German-speaking lands soared exponentially. But the year 1854, when Raabe commenced writing *Die Chronik der Sperlingsgasse*, turned out to be the worst of all. The emigrations of that peak year surpassed every previous exodus of Germans seeking relief from pauperism.

Such was the desperate state of affairs in the German-speaking world when Raabe began to compose this novel. Doubtless, he had been greatly moved by what he saw, for when he took up his pen to write this chronicle, he addressed himself, first of all, to the terrible conditions existing in Germany. In the very opening lines of the novel we read about scarcity and dearth, about the need, sickness, and sorrow of the populace: "It is a bad age indeed! Laughter has become dear. . . . In the distance roll the dark and bloody thunderclouds of war, while, closer-by, disease, hunger, and misery have laid their gloomy veil over the entire area round about. . . ."[25] The further we read in the novel, the more we realize that contemporary allusions of this sort become basic to its structure. The emigrants fleeing to the United States and elsewhere, for instance, can be seen again and again, and the narrator's commentary gives clearly the reasons for their taking to flight:

No longer is it the old German sense of adventure and wanderlust which drives people away from hearth and home, cities and countryside, which tears the charcoal burner away from his forest, and the miner away from his dark shaft, which pulls the shepherd down from his Alpine meadows, and which lets them all depart together for the Far West: distress, misery, and oppression are now the things which scourge our citizens and which force them to leave their homeland, with bleeding hearts.[26]

In such passages the narrator seems to speak with the seasoned authority of a sad observer of contemporary reality; the drama of 1848 and, more particularly, its tragic aftereffects as felt in 1854 have become a central concern for him.

But if the narrator seems to be seeking the truth about reality in his "age of revolution" (as we read on the novel's last page), the peculiar thing about this novel is that the commentary on the times is confided to the reader by means of a fabricated diary. As was the case with Ludwig's novel, so here too the fictional technique of reminiscence comes into play. The stirring picture of reality in the early post-1848 years appears wrapped in the fictional garb of personal recollection, and fact becomes interwoven with fiction. The theme of reality and imagination, which had been so prominent in *Zwischen Himmel und Erde*, thus is projected in Raabe's novel as well. But basic formal differences also exist between Raabe's and Ludwig's treatment of this theme. *Zwischen Himmel und Erde* is an autobiographical novel, *Die Chronik der Sperlingsgasse* a diary novel. In the former, the narrator is shown turning memory into reality by feigning to be an autobiographer; in the latter, the narrator makes believe he is a diarist, offering reality in the fictional form of his daily entries. In Ludwig's novel, a fictional autobiographer recalls those happenings of yesteryear which had most markedly shaped the course of his life; in Raabe's novel, a fictional diarist records all sorts of unrelated events and thoughts which he experienced over a briefer period of time. Raabe's narrative diarist is prompted by an interest in particular time units (seasons of the year, months, days, hours) and is moved by a faith greater than that of Ludwig's autobiographer in the efficacy of delineating such concise time units.

The form of the diary novel, accordingly, gives Raabe's narrator the advantage (over his counterpart in Ludwig's novel) of pretending to come closer to reality. A diary does not recall a reality that has become blurred, partially forgotten, or distorted by the quirks of a fallible memory; nor is it a belated attempt at self-justification, a mutation of the past, a malicious attempt to remold history in order to bolster and exalt the autobiographer's ego. Instead, it constitutes the more faithful recording of a specific event on the very day it occurred; the moment's happenings are committed to paper in their immediacy, before they have had a chance to become blurred, partly forgotten or distorted, before they have been deliberately truncated and manipulated in the light of subsequent experiences. Since the diary is written ostensibly for the eyes of the diarist alone, little or no attempt need be made to varnish the account of the past to make the recorder look better than he actually was. All in all, the diary form of recollection endows Raabe's novel with a far greater concern for fidelity to reality than was the case in the autobiographical reminiscences at the heart of Ludwig's novel. A reader of both works quickly notices that the precise dates and specific geographical and historical references in Raabe's diary stand out in marked contrast to the conspicuous absence of such in Ludwig's novel.

But if it can be maintained that the narrator of Raabe's novel, by resorting to the medium of a diary to tell the story, seeks to create the impression of scrupulous authenticity and sincerity in his portrayal of real life, if he is most anxious to let the reader know that it is reality, and not fiction, which he is depicting—"I am not writing a novel," he states in his first entry—then it must be countered that the diary form of this novel appears more affected than genuine. The diarist here only *pretends* to record the random happenings of

life on a diurnal basis; actually, he skips over many days and ma-
nipulates his entries to suit his fictional purposes. The absence of
regular day-by-day notations renders the diary form perfunctory,
then, and the narrative moves noticeably into the realm of fiction.
The narrator proves himself too great a master of the art of omission
to convince us thoroughly that he is confiding the contents of his
personal diary to us. Despite all his pretenses at setting forth his
daily life on paper, the most convincingly factual and homely details
about the diarist's family, love life, daily meals, indeed daily work,
remain undisclosed. New Year's Eve is allowed to come and go, yet
the diarist records nothing of what he experienced. The same holds
true for the Easter holidays, which are likewise conspicuously
omitted. The intimate revelations of the narrator's passions seem
lacking; there are hardly any candid expressions, no honest record
of personal obsessions, of successes or failures, no genuine echo of
scorn or complaint. For a personal diary, there is an altogether
strange omission of inner life; and of course there are no "sweet
nothings," no such vapid but realistic notes as "nothing important
happened today." In short, we scarcely perceive a human being
with a heart that beats and blood that flows.

In addition to these gaps, certain entries strain the bounds of
probability, such as the story of the actress who must leave the
bedside of her dying child for the theater so that the show may go
on, and who, when the performance is over, rushes home to witness
the child's death just as she arrives. It is scarcely credible that the
child waits to die until the very moment of the mother's return.
Purely fabricated, furthermore, are such mundane details as the
date given in the diary for the celebration of the queen's birthday:
February 28; in fact, the birthday of Queen Consort Elisabeth of
Prussia fell on November 13.

Thus the diary form of this novel is employed, on the one hand,
as an index of extraordinary fidelity to reality in the revolutionary
age; yet, on the other hand, the same diary form finds itself transformed into a piece of pure fiction. Reality is rendered into full art;
conversely, fiction is made to seem real. Is *Die Chronik der Sper-*
lingsgasse truly a work of fiction, or does the narrator's disclaimer
(that he is not writing a novel) hold true? Should Raabe's reader
react to this diary as if it were a real record, or as a fictional statement? The margin between fact and fabrication has become tenuous
indeed; and that, surely, constitutes the most disquieting truth
about life that this diary—this novel—wishes to convey.

Before we take leave of *Die Chronik der Sperlingsgasse*, it should be noted that when Raabe published his novel, he did not have his real name printed on the title page, but rather the name of a fictitious author: Jacob Corvinus. Why did Raabe use a pseudonym? He had no good reason, as far as we know, for concealing his true identity. Strengthened by the absence of any such reason, we would venture to say that just as this novel's diary form points to the perplexity in differentiating between the real and the imaginary, so the fictionalizing of the very author himself enhances the reader's difficulty in distinguishing between fact and fabrication.

III *Gottfried Keller*

The novel *Der grüne Heinrich* (Green Henry), written, revised, and rewritten by Gottfried Keller throughout most of the entire era of German Poetic Realism, sank its roots as deeply into Keller's gruesome revolutionary experiences of 1848–1849 as did the best of his novellas and lyrics. When the novel finally appeared in 1879 and 1880, its sheer length (comprising four volumes with a total of 1,364 pages) dwarfed everything else Poetic Realism had produced. Upon its completion, Keller became the most respected author of his time in Central Europe. The Danish critic Georg Brandes lost no time in proclaiming him "the greatest living German writer."[27] In addition to his superbly inventive novellas and exquisite lyrics, Keller had now composed the mightiest novel of the epoch. No other German Poetic Realist could claim to have excelled in all three of the movement's literary genres. When Keller died ten years later, this novel was already basking in the sunshine of its eighth edition. By the year 1919, the year before the copyright expired, it had succeeded in arousing so much public interest that it could be read in its one-hundredth edition.

But the novel was not only widely read and appreciated by the public; the best critics of the day, too, were consistent in their praise of it. Julian Schmidt was one of the first to recognize its uncommon qualities. He quickly labeled an early version, printed in 1854 and 1855, as one of the most ingenious books that had been written in years, the work of an extraordinarily talented novelist.[28] Theodor Storm became so intrigued by it that he reread it annually for the rest of his life.[29] Theodor Fontane considered it the crowning achievement of Keller's entire career as a writer.[30] In recent times, Thomas Mann has referred to it as "a book altogether out of the

ordinary" and one which "I read with the greatest pleasure and
sympathy, with ever growing admiration for the cleanly displayed
wealth of vitality . . . [and for] the delicious precision of its language."[31]

Only three years after this *magnum opus* appeared, it was translated into Danish, the language of the literature which, despite
striking differences, was most closely aligned to German Poetic
Realism. Keller wrote to his translator in Copenhagen (the versatile
poet Holger Drachmann, 1846–1908), stating, for the benefit of his
Danish readers, that he had, on the one hand, written an autobiographical novel, but that he had also reworked the facts of his life
quite freely; the autobiography contained inventions and alterations
added for fictional purposes. The stories about his childhood and
school days were essentially true to fact, he said, whereas those
about his love affairs were all fictitious.[32] This confession is significant, for it reveals how much he wished it known that the novel
constituted a *real* record of his early life and yet showed a deliberately *poetic* reflection of it. The medley of fact and fiction which
had resounded from Ludwig's autobiographical and Raabe's diary
novel continues, and the same two dramatic components of Keller's
earlier novella *Romeo und Julia auf dem Dorfe* reappear now in
new guise.

Nowhere in this novel do these dual sounds orchestrate as well,
perhaps, as in those passages which—if we are to believe Keller's
words—had been most thoroughly contrived: the ones pertaining
to love affairs. Invented as these love scenes would appear to be
in the autobiography, they represent nevertheless the genuine ache
of mature love in the life of Heinrich, the novel's hero; and as such
they certainly constitute the most important phase of his entanglement with reality. Indeed, it is the real experience of love which
makes the boy shed the green bark that must be relinquished before
he can embrace full manhood (the point in his life, incidentally,
where the autobiographer breaks off the account). Heinrich's sam-
pling of love, however, becomes as discordant as the variance between fact and fiction in the whole of the first-person novel. Lithe
as a dancer, we learn, Heinrich flits simultaneously between two
women: the spiritual, ethereal Anna, to whom he feels drawn for
idealistic reasons rather than because of any sensual inclination, and
Judith, who awakens in him the itch for carnal adventure but fails
to satisfy his longing for a more uplifting relationship. Each woman

embodies the opposite side of his entanglement with love, the one proffering the ennobling qualities necessary for his spiritual welfare, the other arousing his natural desire for physical passion. Essentially Heinrich, in tasting love, is torn between the two counterparts of his quest for feminine affection. The key sentence telling us this is poised, fittingly, at the very center of the novel, in the last paragraph at the end of its first half: "I felt that I was torn in two, and I wanted to hide myself from Anna with Judith, and from Judith with Anna."

This sentence, anchored so centrally in the autobiographical novel of fact and fiction, touches the heart of Heinrich's twin exposure to love. These relationships are so contrived, and yet are meant to appear so real, that the question naturally arises: which of these two women in Heinrich's life offers the real love, which the love of his dream world? Ostensibly, the love for Anna is the more genuine. She is the woman who matters most to Heinrich; his love for her proves to be more enduring, as Heinrich finally withdraws his affection for Judith in favor of Anna. Hence, the shorter-lived love for Judith would seem to represent more the fantasy-dreams of Heinrich's masculine instincts than a true love. This love, for all its sensual attraction, is never really consummated; Heinrich even refuses to call his affection for her love, and he cannot bring himself to introduce her to his family as the one he loves. This love lacks commitment and is, consequently, no real love at all.

But if it may be claimed that the narrator's love for Anna is more genuine and that his love for Judith hardly rises above the level of his sexual longings, it must also be said—with no less force—that his love for Anna is altogether unnatural and rather unreal. Since Heinrich does not love Anna as a man would a woman, his feeling of attachment lacks the rich relationship necessary to make it truly abiding. His love for Judith, however, is wholly natural, as it arises from an immediate, mutual attraction and possesses spontaneous vitality. Heinrich appears to be as genuinely infatuated with her as she is with him. It could be said, therefore, that this constitutes a more real love than the one for Anna.

Side by side with the scenes of love, which Keller called the most complete products of his poetic imagination, he placed those other episodes in which he eased into the sovereign leisure of autobiographical fact. These more genuine portions of the novel retrace the flow of Heinrich's early life and bring him up to the threshold of maturity without the benefit of erotic experience. As such, these

sections of the novel—in spite of Keller's statement to the contrary—are more unreal, in a sense, than those describing the love
affairs which, after all, were crucial for the actual transformation of
Heinrich from boy to man. Taking Keller's comment to his Danish
audience literally, the scenes outside the scope of Heinrich's erotic
experiences constitute, in another sense, the ones closest to fact.
Whether more or less real, however, these portions of the novel
likewise reveal Heinrich performing his capers on an extremely thin
tightrope stretched between reality and fantasy.

Just as the hero vacillates between two female characters created
by Keller in the most fictional strands of the novel, so in the nonfictional autobiographical scenes Heinrich moves between two juxtaposed geographic centers on the map of Europe: the verdant
countryside of his native Switzerland and—after the taste of love
has made him shed his green bark—the strange, foreign Bavarian
capital city of Munich.

In Switzerland Heinrich mingles with the rugged landfolk who
derive their subsistence as herdsmen and tillers of the soil. These
are the people who keep in close contact with nature, with the
changes of seasons, with sunshine and rain, with times of sowing
and harvest; they hardly ever lose sight of the hard realities of
existence. They form a sober commonwealth of practical persons
devoid of romanticism, whose aspirations rarely rise beyond the
preservation and increase of their own material goods. All flights
of idealism, all imaginative subtleties seem lacking; instead, the
practical affairs of everyday reality, especially haggling over money,
occupy men's leisure hours. Heinrich, a native of this world, is not
entirely at home in it. His real calling in life, he feels, is to be an
artist; and so he separates himself from the Swiss rural setting and
betakes himself to the "city of the arts": Munich. There his imaginative nature, his lack of real stability, the fullness of his fantasy,
and the intensity of his subjective emotion would be able to find
a more compatible abode. If the sturdy farmers of Switzerland present themselves as more elemental than imaginative, the citizenry
of the glittering royal capital of Bavaria is so thoroughly smothered
by the artificialities of civilization that it no longer has any roots in
reality. Elaborate festivals, exclusive masquerade balls, the splendor of the royal court, patriotic fervor devoid of practical reasoning,
and, above all, the Bohemian world of the artist take precedence
in this city where Heinrich seeks to become assimilated. He wishes

to identify himself with a wholly abstract world, centered around a fictional preoccupation with the improbable and with the fancies of the grotesque. Heinrich's paintings, accordingly, become more and more abstract and eventually lose all contact with reality.

But which geographic setting portrays the real world of Heinrich? His native Switzerland, whose extreme practicality never satisfies his imaginative longings and where he never really feels at home? Or this fairy-tale-like Bavaria, where his abstract paintings so thoroughly ignore real life that they do not "sell" and he cannot earn a living? Ostensibly, the granite of his Swiss Alps holds the stronger attraction for him, for it is to that world that he returns. In Munich he lives on thin air, wastes his time, and gets into debt; upon leaving, he sees himself as a mental and moral failure. Yet, when he returns to Switzerland he·hardly finds any reality to which he can assent. Roots are not really established. It is with no absorbing interest that he goes about the business of earning his daily livelihood. He remains unanchored in any real family life, and his passions lack vitality. Significantly, the Swiss society which he has, on the surface, rejoined becomes as fictitious as it is devoid of actual political and social conflicts, mercantile enterprises, banks, factories, or productive pastures. The reader wonders whether Heinrich might be merely sustaining himself in a Switzerland more artificial than real. In Munich, by way of contrast, he had involved himself in a genuinely throbbing life; in addition, that life corresponded more to his real interests.

Reality and artificiality, hence, appear as intensely intertwined in the autobiography's nonfictional parts as they were in the fictional strands of the novel. In truth and in fiction, the identical twin notes sound again and again; indeed, both become so generously and subtly compounded that the reader continually loses track of which of the two he is experiencing.

The most striking feature of this fictional autobiography, however, is that it begins and ends with death: death encircles the entire chronicle of truth and distortion. No reader can fail to be struck by the extent to which the aura of death permeates the novel's opening paragraph:

The little cemetery surrounding the church—the latter's whitewash still glowing despite its age—has never been extended; its soil consists literally of the dissolved bones of previous generations. It is impossible that even to a depth of ten feet there could be a grain of that soil that has not undertaken its journey through the human organism and that has not helped, at some time in the past, to plow over the rest of the soil. But I am exaggerating and forgetting the four pinewood boards which go into the ground at each new burial, and which spring from an equally ancient race of giant trees growing on the verdant hills round about. I am forgetting, furthermore, the coarse, honest linen of the shrouds which grew in these fields, which was spun and bleached here, which belongs to the family just as much as the pinewood boards, and which does not prevent the soil of our churchyard from being just as pleasantly cool and black as any other. The greenest of grass grows here; and roses, together with jasmine, proliferate in such heavenly disorder and exuberance that there is no need to plant individual shrubs on any new grave, for every grave has to be dug out of a forest of flowers, and only the gravedigger knows precisely where, in this chaos, the tract begins that has to be dug anew.[33]

In the novel's closing sequences, death looms even larger. The penultimate chapter dwells upon the burial preparations for the narrator's mother, just deceased, as well as upon the darkness in his life which followed as soon as "the grave of my poor dear mother was closed." The final chapter tells of his living death thereafter. He lives out the rest of his life quietly and obscurely in unpretentious but regular employment. This sorrowful existence goes on "without the hope of a brighter life." Everything he observes is "tinged with gloom." Finally realizing that this is "no life," he wishes to escape. But he cannot; he meets again the robust, sensuous Judith—the woman for whom he once felt such passion—and decides to remain near her. They renounce, however, "what the world calls happiness," forego "making themselves man and wife," and continue to see each other only as cousins, "sometimes daily, sometimes weekly, sometimes only once in a year." This love turns sterile, this life loses its vitality—a living death. Significantly, the autobiography is not continued beyond the time when the narrator discovers he is only interring himself in this living death (he is still a comparatively young man when he stops chronicling the events of his life). There can be no prospects for a viable future.

The somberness and despondency felt at the novel's beginning and end sharpen our sensitivity to an ominous note of discord between the contrapuntal instruments of truth and fiction that play their music throughout the vast symphony of this autobiographical novel; and it is the futility of resolving the discordance, we finally gather, that remains the prevailing tone of this ingenious but enigmatic work.

The earliest published version of the novel found an extension in real life when a Prussian privy councillor by the name of Wilhelm Petersen (1835–1900) saw himself mirrored in Keller's fictional Heinrich. "I am a sort of Grüner Heinrich," he wrote in a letter to Keller.[34] This Prussian official vacillated most of his life between an apparently highly successful career in public service and an unfulfilled dream to devote himself completely to art.

To read the obituaries of Wilhelm Petersen is to receive the firm impression that his public service was truly exemplary and that he was blessed with singular good fortune all his life. A regular and steady advancement in the Prussian civil service, the honor and respect given to him by those in the community he served, a loving family life—those were the fruits of his untiring labors in a society whose principles he fully condoned.

But Petersen's life also had another dimension, which is documented in his extensive correspondences with Keller, Storm, and other writers.[35] He possessed a creative spirit that was unwilling to let itself be regulated by the timetables of social responsibility. He longed for the bright color of a Bohemian world and the more exhilarating atmosphere of a life freed from the shackles of convention. He felt that his career in the civil service enslaved him to a suffocating straitjacket of facts, deeds, and practicalities; that his espousal of the ethics of bureaucratic hard work divorced him from the refreshment of art. "Life without art," he said in one of his letters to Keller, "is but a shadow, empty and desolate." To Storm he wrote: "Only a life that is artistically creative is worth living." The stifling mechanism of bureaucracy left little room, however, for the flights of imagination he so avidly desired. Hence, he keenly felt the irritating dullness of his humdrum existence and remained unable to accommodate himself inwardly to his pragmatic life as a public official. Even as a very young man he had not wished to be tied down in an unpoetic world of communal security. Nor had he wanted to assume the responsibilities of family life. The freedom of the poet and painter attracted him more. That he did not follow the dictates of his imaginative disposition was due to parental pressure. But even though he was destined to meet his obligations within the conventional round of life, his gaze always remained secretly fixed on the life he could not overtly lead. Anonymously, he published poetry in journals of the day. When official duties were not clamoring for his attention, he would paint and model with clay. He allowed himself the luxury of frequent and expensive rail travel to visit Keller and other writers, and he bestowed lavish gifts upon them, forcing the members of his own family to contend with a more meager income than normally would have accrued to them by virtue of the fact that the paterfamilias enjoyed the salary of a Prussian privy councillor.

Recognition, however, did not come to Petersen for his activity in the arts. His verse, his paintings, and his sculptures never received more than scant praise and were quickly forgotten. In contrast, his professional accomplishments were duly recorded (in glowing terms of admiration) in the annals of the Prussian civil service. But which constituted the real world for Petersen, which the artificial and empty one?

The frustration of reaping unwanted success in the public sector while seeing any concomitant reward in the poetic world he longed for stifled, led Petersen to start a fictional chronicle of his life—in glib imitation of *Der grüne Heinrich*—but this attempt to project the genuinely felt discord in his life into an autobiographical novel proved as illusive as his other attempts at art. If the conflict between his public and private self could not be resolved in the real world, it could not be harmonized in fiction either.

Only one other option remained open for the civil servant. The original version of Keller's novel, which Petersen had mentally translated into his personal reality, could be tempered by facts taken from his own life and presented to the reader in a new, more persuasive form, one more closely related to actual experience. This is precisely what occurred. Keller, on the dogged insistence of the civil servant/artist, deftly brought a further aspect of reality into the novel which had meant so much to Petersen; and when the work appeared in its revised edition of 1879–1880, it became, in its closing chapters, the fictionally disguised portrait of the twin faces of Wilhelm Petersen. The living death of Heinrich with which the novel breaks off, in particular, reflects the mature wisdom of the practical official who knew that the abysmal disjunction of his public and private lives would remain unreconciled for as long as he lived.

Keller never tired of recounting the debt he owed to his Prussian Heinrich. When he was approaching death, he expressed the wish to see the wise bureaucrat Petersen—the frustrated artist—once more. The latter immediately left his official duties in the town of Schleswig near the Prussian-Danish frontier and made the long trip to Zurich in order to be close, one last time, to the ailing author of the novel which he believed to be "without equal in the world."[36]

CHAPTER 5

The Recession of German
Poetic Realism

I The Passing of the Forty-Eighters

JULIAN SCHMIDT, the heroic founder of the movement launched in 1848, died on March 27, 1886. The loud, polemic voice of the most important critic to have appeared on the German literary scene in more than half a century, since the brothers August Wilhelm Schlegel (1767–1845) and Friedrich Schlegel (1772–1829), boomed forth no longer. On the following day, the leading newspaper of Berlin, the *Vossische Zeitung*, ran an editorial saying that even Schmidt's opponents would have to concede that a spirit of tremendous force had now been silenced. The *Times* of London, announcing the death of Schmidt on March 30, 1886, spoke of him as the "Nestor of German literary historians." He had set German Poetic Realism on the course that determined its basic principles; his theory of literature had given the movement its historical cohesion. Allegiance to his literary revolution of 1848, either expressed or implied, formed the unbroken red thread that ran through the masterpieces of the movement.

With the chief pilot of the movement gone, it became easy for new modes of literature to establish themselves on German soil and to take the place of Poetic Realism, indeed to supersede it completely. A scant two months after Schmidt's death in Berlin, a literary club (formed in the same city with the name *Durch*) successfully drew followers together to proclaim a more modern form of literary expression. In the following year, the club's main organizer, Eugen Wolff (1863–1929), issued a set of ten guidelines for the reform of German literature. The concerns of the Forty-Eighters had become things of the past.

118

One by one, the other Forty-Eighters, too, passed from the scene, and that further hastened the recession of German Poetic Realism. Storm died in 1888, soon after having completed his novella *Der Schimmelreiter* (The Rider on the White Horse). Keller died two years later. Ludwig's leadership in the movement had ended abruptly with his premature death in 1865. Meyer, the poet of the movement who may have been least directly touched by the fires of 1848, saw himself forced by ill health to terminate his poetic career soon after completing his novella *Angela Borgia* in 1891; seven final years of literary famine were to follow. Groth lived on until 1899, but he added nothing of importance to *Quickborn* after its fourteenth edition of 1883. Raabe, the youngest of the literary giants of 1848, continued the longest as an active writer. His last completed work, *Hastenbeck*, was published in 1898. But this date is misleading—if not totally irrelevant—since the junior member of German Poetic Realism's elite had actually been the first to leave its ranks. Soon after finishing his immensely successful *Chronik der Sperlingsgasse*, he tried his hand at writing tendentious fiction, a shift in emphasis which resulted in an arid moralizing novel published in 1864 with the title *Der Hungerpastor* (The Hunger Pastor). Thus, though later in his long career he came to embrace a more conspicuously modern craft of fiction—which was not without its merit—his defection from the camp of Poetic Realism became permanent when he embarked on the literary path that led to *Der Hungerpastor*.

In sum, it can be said that by 1891 defection, disease, and death had claimed every one of the commanding figures of the movement. Moreover, no new leaders could be expected to arise from the generation born after 1848, for whom the revolutionary era possessed little more than historical significance. Clearly, an epoch in literature was drawing to a close.

II   *Theodor Fontane*

Yet, great movements in literature die hard, and for the death knell to ring over German Poetic Realism it took more than just the passing of its august leadership. The movement received a more fatal blow when another Forty-Eighter, who had always been closely associated with the literature of the age—without, however, ever having risen to a position of eminence in it—suddenly grasped the slack reins of leadership during the last decade of the century and guided the movement into a direction totally foreign to it. This new leader in the era's twilight was none other than Theodor Fontane, whose name we have mentioned so many times in tracing the history of the movement.

Born in 1819, Fontane was a true contemporary of Schmidt (b.1818), Storm (1817), Keller (1819), Groth (1819), Ludwig (1813), and Meyer (1825). He knew several of them personally and thoroughly familiarized himself with their writings. His experiences in the revolutionary upheavals of 1848, moreover, had been as ghastly and sobering as anything the others had seen. During the worst fighting in the streets of Berlin in 1848, he had helped man the barricades and had been an eyewitness to much of the death and destruction there. With avid interest and personally felt passion, he had followed the effects and aftereffects of the insurrections in Prussia and in the Danish duchies of Schleswig and Holstein. Again and again his indignation had been sorely aroused.

All of these things prepared Fontane well for a career in Poetic Realism, and it was not long before he identified himself more formally with the movement by writing lyric verse which was wholly compatible with it. Recognition did not remain lacking, either: the important critical anthologies of Echtermeyer-Masius, Scherer, and Storm each included selections from his poetry. Storm, especially, found warm words of praise for "this newly born singer."[1]

A number of Fontane's poems, in particular those in which he succeeded in poetically linking the rhythm of balladry with the realism of current events, belong among the finest treasures that the movement produced, but Fontane came closest to being a remarkable Poetic Realist, perhaps, when he composed his compelling poem "Ausgang" (Exit) in 1889:

> Immer enger, leise, leise,
> Ziehen sich die Lebenskreise,
> Schwindet hin, was prahlt und prunkt,
> Schwindet Hoffen, Hassen, Lieben,
> Und ist nichts in Sicht geblieben
> Als der letzte dunkle Punkt.[2]

> (Now life's circles gently, lightly,
> Dwindle ever, draw in slightly;
> Vanish all display and show,

Vanish hoping, loving, hating;
And there stays in view but waiting
The dark point at last to know.)

Translated by C. Fillingham Coxwell[3]

The poem lies clearly in the great lyric tradition of Storm, Groth, Keller, and Meyer. It gathers its nourishment from that tradition and, for its part, confirms and strengthens that tradition. It offers another chilling meditation on the ephemerality of life, for the specter of human transience again looms up on the dark poetic horizon of approaching death. Life is captured in a single sentence, in a single stanza. One hears in the background, poetically audible in the steady stream of trochaic beats, the incessant march of time's invisible feet moving unerringly onward to the clearly visible terminus of death. The regularly paced rhythm of trochees steps out of cadence in the last line, marking that dark point of death where man reaches his final destiny and all life is transformed. The brevity of these verses further underlines the brief duration of man's stay on earth. The truth about the ever-narrowing circle of interests and activities in life appears as ruthless as it is compactly stated; yet for all its uncompromising directness, it is no less poetic, and the splendor of its plaintive sincerity possesses genuine lyrical sensitivity. In short, this poem of Fontane is a masterpiece of Poetic Realism.

Distinguished as Fontane's contributions to the lyric of Poetic Realism were, however, his verse alone was not destined to bring him fame. He also produced a dazzling array of novels that have come to overshadow his accomplishments as a lyricist. But the novels added a dimension to Poetic Realism that was fundamentally alien to it, and thus they had the effect of supplanting it. For Fontane abandoned the memorializing and autobiographical novel of German Poetic Realism in favor of a novel of social forces; man in relation to society became the chief concern of his writing. What Fontane offered were fictional portraits of human beings interlocked in an existing social order and acting in response to the dictates of social custom.[4]

As such, these novels are heavily influenced, of course, by the heritage of the Forty-Eighters. When Fontane tells us of the inexorability of society's pressures on his characters, he certainly moves among the realities of life. Like the other major German authors of his generation, he, too, allows a thoroughly entrenched realism to preside over the execution of his novels. An evocation of a holistic social world proves no less realistic than a description of man's preoccupation with his own life in relation to death, with genuineness and artificiality in individual existence, with what is actually true and what is merely the product of the imagination. Fontane's realism, like that of his fellow Forty-Eighters, distinguishes itself by a felicity of poetic expression. His novels constitute strikingly moving poetic creations, which transfigure the wearisome prose of everyday life into fictional realities of universal validity. Both in their genuine realism and in their poetic brilliance, therefore, they have much in common with Poetic Realism; and it was no less a champion of the movement than Conrad Ferdinand Meyer who confirmed this affinity. Speaking of Fontane's landmark novel *Unwiederbringlich* (Beyond Recall), he called it notable for its highly true-to-life characters and its concomitant poetic spirit.[5]

Yet, the similarity to Poetic Realism is deceptive. In the final analysis, Fontane's novels are only heirs to Poetic Realism and not representative of it. Instead of focusing on an intensely personal search for the reality of individual lives, as did his fellow Forty-Eighters, Fontane concentrates on social relationships. The flair for social nuances, however, was foreign to Poetic Realism. "God forbid," Julian Schmidt once said, "that the novel should attempt to solve social questions."[6] Indeed, such novels of *mœurs* placed Fontane's fiction—as Thomas Mann once remarked in a lecture given at Princeton—back into the mainstream of the social novels of England, France, and Russia during the nineteenth century.[7] By adding a distinct social dimension to his Poetic Realism, therefore, Fontane departed from the literary tradition of 1848 and turned German fiction toward a new direction.

Significantly, Fontane's most incisive thrust forward to a new novel of social awareness, more European than German, coincided precisely with the passing of the leadership in German Poetic Realism and the faltering of that movement, or, to use Fontane's own words, just when German fiction had lapsed into "a void with the deaths of Keller and Storm."[8] Fontane's new beginning found its clearest expression—as Peter Demetz has cogently argued—when the pivotal social novel *Unwiederbringlich* appeared in 1891.[9] That was also the exact year in which Poetic Realism's final landmark, Meyer's novella *Angela Borgia*, was printed. With the advent of *Unwiederbringlich*, a historic era in German literature became irretrievable. Quite intentionally, we know, Fontane transferred the setting of this new novel away from Germany to the landscape of Denmark.[10] On the miraculously fertile literary soil of Denmark (to use a striking image of Oskar Seidlin[11]), Fontane succeeded in finding a new springtide for German literature.

Energetically and imaginatively, hence, Fontane stepped into the void created by the passing of his fellow Forty-Eighters; but when he transformed the doctrine of Poetic Realism into one of Social Realism, he also rang down the curtain on the literary movement that had sprung up in 1848.

CHAPTER 6

Conclusion

I N THE foregoing chapters it has been my concern to survey the origins and course of the movement in German literature known as Poetic Realism: how it began, how it progressed, and how it eventually came to an end. The main concentration has been on its most enduring and superlative literary achievements, those masterpieces of creative vitality which we can single out and interpret in the light of the reception accorded them over the past 130 years. Our knowledge of this reception and the perspective it permits is one of the distinct benefits of being able to look back at the movement from the vantage point of a century later.

Some readers of this book may be surprised that it has sought to comprehend Poetic Realism as a "movement" rather than a "period" in German literary history. It has been, however, a specific intention of this study to draw attention to the fact that German Poetic Realism was launched as a movement in literature through the critical efforts of Julian Schmidt. Nowhere else has it been argued with as much vigor that the masterpieces of German Poetic Realism constitute conscious or unconscious tributes to Schmidt's literary revolution of 1848. He was the apostle, the prophet, and the mediator who succeeded in making new ideas live in Germany, and who inspired his contemporaries to a literature that was different from what had gone before. To overlook his literary program as the sure foundation on which German Poetic Realism rests is to define the term ambiguously, to blur the outlines of the movement, and to regard Poetic Realism as a catchword for everything that German writers of the mid-nineteenth century produced.

Such a loose conception of the movement is wrong. Those works written prior to the watershed of 1848—and even some of the early post-1848 literature conceived by writers solidly rooted in the pre-1848 age—do not belong to the new movement inaugurated by

124

Schmidt. Furthermore, not all German writers who fit within the particular section of time we have ascribed to German Poetic Realism can be categorized as Poetic Realists. In the post-1848 age there existed, for instance, two crosscurrents, one assenting to reality and another retreating from it. For within its own time, German Poetic Realism produced its antithesis: a countermovement which turned away from the vast and raging torrents of real life and found shelter on an isle of artificial beauty.

In comparison with Poetic Realism, this new aestheticism constituted only a very minor literary movement. Nevertheless, among its adherents were two writers who were widely read at that time: Emanuel Geibel (1815–1884) and Paul Heyse (1830–1914). With Heyse, the countermovement found its culmination. Fontane clearly recognized this when, in 1890, he likened Heyse's role in German literature to the place in history dominated by the ancient ruler King Polycrates. In a letter to Heyse, Fontane stated: "You stood at the helm for thirty years, so prominently that your literary epoch will very probably bear your name."[1] Heyse's renown abroad, too, bespoke his position of preeminence. He was elected to membership in the American Philosophical Society, an honor rarely bestowed on a foreign writer. In England, the Royal Society of Literature made him an Honorary Foreign Fellow. The Swedish Academy awarded him the Nobel Prize for Literature.

Like so many of the German Poetic Realists, Heyse, too, had been profoundly moved by the events of 1848. Writing to Geibel from Berlin on March 20, 1848, he had said: "I have never been so agitated in my life. . . . I can understand the anger. I have seen the corpses lying in front of the City Hall, young and seemingly robust bodies, soiled with blood, a hole in the chest or the skull. . . ."[2] But if Heyse had been horrified by the events of the revolution, this shock did not impel him, as a writer, to embrace a form of literature consonant with Schmidt's program. On the contrary, instead of attempting to grapple with the essence of reality, he sedulously avoided it. He fled from the acceptance of the tragic experience brought on by revolution and sought comfort in the static peace of artifice. The countermovement which he, Geibel, and a host of pallid imitators represented was one of overt escapism.

It did not take long, of course, for the founder of German Poetic Realism to repudiate this obvious evasion of reality, and it was only natural that Schmidt should single out the most conspicuous oracle of this hedonistic literary movement as the particular target for repeated assault: again and again he took issue with Heyse in the *Grenzboten*.[3] In 1869 and 1872 he felt himself driven to denounce Heyse's deceptive idealism in essays printed elsewhere as well.[4] Heyse was ridiculed by statements such as the following: "Heyse's literature lies nestled in a nice little peaceful valley removed from it all. . . . In order to please him, Mother Nature is obliged to put on her Sunday dress. . . . Heyse is at home in the land of elves and fairies."[5] Yet, Schmidt's polemics could not belie the fact that two opposing literary movements had sprung up in Germany in the post-1848 age. Indeed, his derision of Heyse's aestheticism only served to call public attention as much to its presence as to its folly. There could, consequently, no longer be any doubt about it: two currents flowed through German literature after 1848, a major one— with its towering figures of Schmidt, Storm, Keller, Meyer, Groth, Ludwig, Raabe—and a minor one led by Heyse and Geibel. Within the same "period" of literary history there existed, side by side, two different "movements"—another good reason for preferring the designation "movement" to "period" when speaking of German Poetic Realism.

In concluding this latest, but surely not last, study of German Poetic Realism, it seems appropriate to point out a genuine desideratum of literary scholarship: the need for comparative studies of the three national voices of Poetic Realism in Denmark, Sweden, and Germany. The attempt to see each of the three movements in the light of the other two could prove as rewarding as viewing each within the historical perspective of its own respective origin.

In different tongues, historians of literature share an interest in a phenomenon of the same name. German literary historians refer to their *Poetischer Realismus*, Danish critics have their *poetisk realisme*, the Swedes their *poetisk realism*. These three literary movements of the same name also have a family likeness, but a likeness which allows for wide divergencies and curious time lags, for in each land this literary phenomenon was conditioned by varying political, social, and critical factors. If in the German-speaking world the genesis of *Poetischer Realismus* was caused by the revolutions of 1848, in Denmark *poetisk realisme* emerged during a period of unprecedented national crisis: the Danish state had declared itself bankrupt in 1813; in the years around 1820 agriculture, industry, and commerce were paralyzed; poverty and despair were visible everywhere. The comprehensive history of Danish literature by P. H. Traustedt et al.—which is considered in Denmark to be the standard work on that nation's literary history—makes it clear that these circumstances were crucial for the advent of *poetisk realisme*.[6] Swedish *poetisk realism*, on the other hand, was not precipitated by any dire politico-social events, but rather developed, as Kurt Aspelin has ably argued, out of an extensive literary debate in the 1830s.[7]

The similarities and differences among these three national manifestations of Poetic Realism should inspire comparative studies. How does Julian Schmidt's campaign to promote the movement in Germany, for instance, compare with the role of Poul Martin Møller (1794–1838) in advancing *poetisk realisme* in Denmark? The standard history of Danish literature in Denmark today recognizes Møller as the chief protagonist of Poetic Realism in his native land. His novella *En dansk Students Eventyr* (The Tale of a Danish Student) is considered to be the first example of *poetisk realisme*. Yet to critics of German Poetic Realism, Møller and his novella are unknown. Another inquiry might profitably be made into the relationship of Storm's poetry and the early verse of the Swedish poet Anders Österling. The latter, captivated by Storm's poetry, once wrote: "The singer Storm will never be forgotten."[8] Scandinavianists regard Österling as an important representative of Swedish Poetic Realism.[9] Is there a connection between Österling's verse and the lyrics of Storm? What attracted this apologist of the verse of Swedish Poetic Realism to Storm's poetry? Where do the lyrics of the German and Swedish branches of Poetic Realism converge? Where do they diverge? Critics have not yet addressed themselves to these and similar questions.

To sum up: a number of points of contact between German Poetic Realism and its twin manifestations in Scandinavia are there to be investigated. Critical inquiries into such areas could help us appreciate more fully the particular character of each national movement and contribute further to the widening of our knowledge of Poetic Realism. It is to be hoped that many such studies will be forthcoming in the future.

Notes and References

Preface

1. Max Weber, *Gesammelte Aufsätze zur Wissenschaftslehre*, 2nd ed. (Tübingen: Mohr, 1951), p. 576.

Chapter One

1. P. H. Traustedt et al., *Dansk Litteratur Historie*, new and enl. ed., III (Copenhagen: Politiken, 1976), pp. 11–22.

2. Cf., in particular, the informative study by Kurt Aspelin, *Poesi och verklighet* (Göteborg: Akademiförlaget, 1967), pp. 20–21, 96–106, 110, 280–81, 283. Also: Elias Bredsdorff, Brita Mortensen, and Ronald Popperwell, *An Introduction to Scandinavian Literature* (Copenhagen: Munksgaard, 1951), pp. 124, 200; Alrik Gustafson, *A History of Swedish Literature* (Minneapolis: University of Minnesota Press, 1961), pp. 224, 237, 280–81, 289, 294, 367, 428, 694.

3. Walter Silz, *Realism and Reality, Studies in the German Novelle of Poetic Realism*, 4th printing (Chapel Hill: University of North Carolina Press, 1965), pp. xiii, 151.

4. E. K. Bennett, *A History of the German Novelle*, 2nd ed., revised and continued by H. M. Waidson (Cambridge, England: Cambridge University Press, 1974), p. 129.

5. Georg Brandes, *Hovedstrømninger i det nittende Aarhundredes Literatur*, 5th revised ed., VI (Copenhagen: Gyldendal, 1924), p. 323.

6. In the studies of Silz and Bennett, Schmidt's name is never mentioned.

7. Henry H. Remak, "The German Reception of French Realism," *PMLA* 69 (1954): 420.

8. Theodor Fontane, *Briefe an Wilhelm und Hans Hertz 1859–1898*, ed. K. Schreinert (Stuttgart: Klett, 1972), p. 198.

9. Ferdinand Lassalle, *Reden und Schriften*, ed. E. Bernstein, III (Berlin: Vorwärts, 1893), p. 613.

10. Wilhelm Dilthey, *Gesammelte Schriften*, 3rd ed., XI (Stuttgart: Teubner; Göttingen: Vandenhoeck & Ruprecht, 1965), p. 234.

11. Gustav Freytag, *Gesammelte Werke*, I (Leipzig: Hirzel, 1887), pp. 162–63.

129

12. *Die Grenzboten*, 1848, II, 253.

13. Ibid., 1848, III, 1–4.

14. Ibid., 1848, III, 154–66.

15. Ibid., 1848, IV, 416–19.

16. Ibid., 1849, I, 237–38.

17. Ibid., 1849, III, 181–86. Ernst Elster, in his edition of Gustav Freytag's *Vermischte Aufsätze* (Leipzig: Hirzel, 1901–1903), attributes this unsigned essay to Freytag rather than to Schmidt, and at least two German dissertations have repeated Elster's assertion. But there is nothing to justify giving Freytag the credit for the essay, since Schmidt, not his coeditor Freytag, was responsible for the journal's literary criticism. Freytag himself said, referring to their joint editorship: "Julian besorgte . . . fast die ganze Literatur und Kunst" (Freytag, *Gesammelte Werke*, I, p. 156). Of course, all of Schmidt's essays in the *Grenzboten* were written in collaboration with his coeditor. But that still does not make Freytag the author.

18. Schmidt continues this argument in a subsequent critique of Auerbach in the *Grenzboten*, 1852, I, 95–102.

19. Ibid., 1850, I, 114–16.

20. Ibid., 1850, I, 5–13.

21. Ibid., 1848, IV, 80.

22. Ibid., 1851, III, 54–57.

23. Gottfried Keller, *Gesammelte Briefe*, ed. C. Helbling, III/1 (Berne: Benteli, 1952), p. 188.

24. *Die Grenzboten*, 1852, II, 41–63.

25. Ibid., 1859, IV, 449.

26. Ibid., 1859, IV, 454.

27. Julian Schmidt, *Geschichte der deutschen Litteratur von Leibniz bis auf unsere Zeit* (Berlin: Hertz, 1896), V, p. 402.

Chapter Two

1. The Twayne World Authors Series has devoted a separate volume to *Theodor Storm*. It was written by A. Tilo Alt (1973).

2. Knud Fabricius, *Sønderjyllands Historie*, IV (Copenhagen: Reitzel, 1936–1937), p. 458.

3. In an address to the House of Commons on April 19, 1848. Printed in *Hansard's Parliamentary Debates*, XCVIII, 514.

4. Schmidt, *Geschichte der deutschen Litteratur von Leibniz bis auf unsere Zeit*, V, p. 462.

5. Reprinted in *Theodor Storms Briefwechsel mit Theodor Mommsen*, ed. H. E. Teitge (Weimar: Böhlau, 1966), pp. 131–41.

6. The most telling narrative of these activities is written in Danish: A. Simonsen, "Theodor Storm og Danmark," *Sønderjydske Aarbøger* 1 (1950): 140–52.

7. *Die Grenzboten*, 1848, IV, 416–19.

8. See Henning Fenger's book on *The Heibergs*, translated for the Twayne World Authors Series by Frederick J. Marker (1971), pp. 143, 152.

9. Modern literary scholarship badly needs a succinct, balanced, readable account of Heiberg's importance as a precursor of the novella of German Poetic Realism. His prefaces in Thomasine Christine Gyllembourg-Ehrensvärd, *Noveller, gamle og nye, af Forf. til "En Hverdags Historie,"* 3 vols. (Copenhagen: Reitzel, 1833) are full of pregnant statements anticipating Storm's theory of the novella. The volumes are rare outside of Denmark. The second edition of this collection, published in 1835, is in the New York Public Library. Volume 3 offers particularly rewarding reading.

10. Georg Lukács, *Soul and Form*, trans. A. Bostock (London: Merlin, 1974), pp. 72–74. Our summary follows, in part, Lukács's brilliant account, which was originally published in German in 1911.

11. Fontane, *Sämtliche Werke*, ed. K. Schreinert et al., XXI/1 (Munich: Nymphenburger Verlagshandlung, 1963), p. 148.

12. Thomas Mann, *Gesammelte Werke* (Frankfurt: Fischer, 1960), XII, 106. Further detail in Günther Weydt, "Thomas Mann und Storm," *Wissenschaft als Dialog*, ed. R. von Heydebrand and K. G. Just (Stuttgart: Metzler, 1969), pp. 182–83.

13. Storm, *Briefe*, ed. P. Goldammer (Berlin and Weimar: Aufbau, 1972), I, 130.

14. *Theodor Storm-Paul Heyse, Briefwechsel. Kritische Ausgabe*, ed. C. A. Bernd, II (Berlin: Erich Schmidt, 1970), p. 119.

15. In an unpublished manuscript, dated January 1962 and now in the Hesse archives of the Schiller-Nationalmuseum in Marbach am Neckar.

16. In the *Athenaeum*, July 7, 1888, p. 16.

17. Keller, *Gesammelte Briefe*, II (1951), p. 454; IV (1954), p. 17.

18. In *Blackwood's Edinburgh Magazine* 64 (1848): 378–79.

19. Ludwig Häusser, *Denkwürdigkeiten zur Geschichte der Badischen Revolution* (Heidelberg: Winter, 1851), pp. 479–598.

20. Keller, *Gesammelte Briefe*, I (1950), pp. 97, 281–83.

21. Ibid., IV, pp. 345–46.

22. Ibid., I, p. 299.

23. Lukács, *Soul and Form*, p. 72.

24. Wolfgang Preisendanz, "Die Keller-Forschung der Jahre 1939–1957," *Germanisch-Romanische Monatsschrift* 39 (1958): 169.

25. In *Allgemeine Zeitung* (Augsburg), April 17, 1856, p. 1722.

26. Schmidt, *Geschichte der deutschen Litteratur von Leibniz bis auf unsere Zeit*, V, p. 577; *Storm-Heyse Briefwechsel*, II, p. 21.

27. Keller, *Gesammelte Briefe*, I, pp. 276–77.

28. G. G. Gervinus, *Shakespeare*, 2nd ed. (Leipzig: Engelmann, 1850), II, p. 3.

29. Keller, *Gesammelte Briefe*, I, pp. 352–53.

30. Cf. Fontane's incisive comment on the two discordant parts: Fontane, *Sämtliche Werke*, XXI/1, pp. 257–58.

31. In *Westminster Review* 14 (1858): 518.

32. The Twayne World Authors Series has devoted a separate volume to *Conrad Ferdinand Meyer*. It was written by Marianne Burkhard (1978).

33. *Conrad Ferdinand Meyer und Julius Rodenberg, Ein Briefwechsel*, ed. A. Langmesser (Berlin: Paetel, 1918), p. 73.

34. Fontane, *Sämtliche Werke*, XXI/1, 327.

35. See Bennett's *History of the German Novelle*, pp. 215–30.

36. In vol. 44 (1879), pp. 608–13. Another essay on Meyer appeared in vol. 53 (1884), pp. 264–83.

37. *Briefe Conrad Ferdinand Meyers*, ed. A. Frey, I (Leipzig: Haessel, 1908), p. 171.

38. *Meyer-Rodenberg Briefwechsel*, p. 64.

39. *Storm-Heyse Briefwechsel*, II (1970), p. 89.

40. Werner Kohlschmidt, *Dichter, Tradition und Zeitgeist* (Berne: Francke, 1965), p. 355.

41. Keller, *Gesammelte Briefe*, III/2 (1953), p. 369; IV (1954), p. 204.

42. *Allgemeine Zeitung* (Munich), April 8, 1887, pp. 1441–42; April 9, 1887, pp. 1450–51.

43. In *Preußische Jahrbücher* 53 (1884): 273.

44. *Briefe Conrad Ferdinand Meyers*, II, p. 130.

Chapter Three

1. *Die Grenzboten*, 1852, IV, 121–32.

2. *Der Briefwechsel zwischen Theodor Storm und Gottfried Keller*, ed. P. Goldammer, 2nd ed. (Berlin and Weimar: Aufbau, 1967), pp. 66, 71.

3. *Schriften der Theodor-Storm-Gesellschaft* 8 (1959): 43.

4. *Die Grenzboten*, 1848, IV, 418.

5. Franz Stuckert, *Theodor Storm* (Bremen: Schünemann, 1955), p. 172.

6. Storm, *Sämtliche Werke*, ed. P. Goldammer, 2nd ed., I (Berlin and Weimar: Aufbau, 1967), pp. 225–26.

7. Storm, *Sämtliche Werke*, ed. A. Köster, VIII (Leipzig: Insel, 1920), p. 154.

8. Alt, *Theodor Storm*, p. 37.

9. For a detailed account of the many revisions of this poem see C. A. Bernd, "Theodor Storms Lyrik," *Nordelbingen* 38 (1969): 104–11.

10. Alt, *Theodor Storm*, p. 46.

11. *Theodor Storm-Eduard Mörike, Theodor Storm-Margarethe Mörike, Briefwechsel. Kritische Ausgabe*, ed. H. and W. Kohlschmidt (Berlin: Erich Schmidt, 1978), p. 30.

12. Fontane, *Sämtliche Werke*, XXI/2, p. 246.

13. Ibid., XXI/2, p. 86.

14. Ibid., XXI/1, p. 498.

15. Mann, *Essays of Three Decades*, trans. H. T. Lowe-Porter (New York: Knopf, 1947), pp. 272–73.

16. Anders Österling, *Dagens gärning* (Stockholm: Bonnier, 1921), p. 169.

17. Manfred Hausmann, "Unendliches Gedicht, Bemerkungen anläßlich der Lyrik Theodor Storms," *Abhandlungen der Akademie der Wissenschaften und der Literatur in Mainz* (1962): 42.

18. Storm had printed this poem in various revisions. The final version, reprinted here, is taken from Storm, *Sämtliche Werke*, ed. A. Köster, I (Leipzig: Insel, 1919), pp. 132–33.

19. From *German Verse from the 12th to the 20th Century in English Translation*, by J. W. Thomas. University of North Carolina Studies in the Germanic Languages and Literatures, No. 44 (Chapel Hill: University of North Carolina Press, 1963), p. 133. Siegfried Mews, the editor of the above-mentioned Studies, has graciously permitted me to change the punctuation at the end of the second line in the third stanza.

20. Kate Freiligrath Kroeker, *A Century of German Lyrics* (London: Heinemann, 1894).

21. Schmidt, *Neue Bilder aus dem geistigen Leben unserer Zeit*, III (Leipzig: Duncker & Humblot, 1873), p. 149.

22. Storm, *Sämtliche Werke*, ed. A. Köster, VIII, p. 86.

23. *Klaus Groths Briefe an seine Braut Doris Finke*, ed. H. Krumm (Braunschweig: Westermann, 1910), p. 238.

24. Groth, *Sämtliche Werke*, I, ed. F. Pauly (Flensburg: Wolff, 1952), p. 24.

25. German text and English translation in *Macmillan's Magazine* 10 (1864): 360.

26. See the graphic account in Groth, *Die patriotische Wirksamkeit eines schleswig-holsteinischen Privatmanns*, ed. V. Pauls (Neumünster: Wachholtz, 1930), pp. 6–14.

27. Geert Seelig, *Klaus Groth, Sein Leben und Werden* (Hamburg: Alster, 1924), p. 113.

28. H. Siercks, *Klaus Groth, Sein Leben und seine Werke* (Kiel: Lipsius & Tischer, 1899), p. 221.

29. C. Rosenberg, "Klaus Groth som plattydsk Digter," *Dansk Maanedsskrift* (1859): II, 121.

30. Groth, *Sämtliche Werke*, VIII, ed. I. Braak and R. Mehlem (Flensburg: Wolff, 1965), p. 260.

31. Seelig, *Klaus Groth, Sein Leben und Werden*, p. 284.

32. *Schriften der Theodor-Storm-Gesellschaft* 4 (1955): 37.

33. Groth, *Gesammelte Werke*, I (Kiel: Lipsius & Tischer, 1893), pp.

117–18. The more recent and more readily available printing of this poem in Groth's *Sämtliche Werke*, II, ed. I. Braak and R. Mehlem (Flensburg: Wolff, 1957), p. 155, is faulty. Hence, the need to quote from the older edition.

34. *Klopstocks sämmtliche Werke*, VII (Leipzig: Göschen, 1823), p. 210.

35. Fontane, *Sämtliche Werke*, XXI/2, p. 743.

36. Keller, *Gedichte* (Heidelberg: Winter, 1846), pp. 43–45.

37. Freiligrath Kroeker, *A Century of German Lyrics*, pp. 177–78.

38. Storm, *Hausbuch aus deutschen Dichtern seit Claudius* (Leipzig: Mauke, 1875), p. 393; G. Scherer, *Deutscher Dichterwald*, 16th ed. (Stuttgart: Deutsche Verlagsanstalt, 1894), p. 274.

39. Freiligrath Kroeker, *A Century of German Lyrics*, p. 177.

40. Keller, *Gesammelte Briefe*, IV, p. 345.

41. Cf. J. M. Lindsay, *Gottfried Keller, Life and Works* (London: Wolff, 1968), p. 105.

42. *Der Briefwechsel zwischen Theodor Storm und Gottfried Keller*, p. 20.

43. *The Penguin Book of German Verse*, ed. L. Forster (latest rpt.: Harmondsworth, England and Baltimore, 1974), pp. 367–69.

44. *German Poetry, A Critical Anthology*, ed. R. M. Browning (latest rpt.: Englewood Cliffs, N.J.: Prentice-Hall, 1975), p. 270.

45. Keller, *Neuere Gedichte* (Braunschweig: Vieweg, 1851), p. 22.

46. Freiligrath Kroeker, *A Century of German Lyrics*, p. 181.

47. Keller, *Gesammelte Briefe*, IV, p. 345.

48. Ibid., IV, p. 34.

49. *Der Briefwechsel zwischen Theodor Storm und Gottfried Keller*, p. 41.

50. Keller, *Gesammelte Gedichte* (Berlin: Hertz, 1883), p. 33.

51. From *Anthology of German Poetry through the 19th Century*, ed. Alexander Gode and Frederick Ungar. Copyright 1964, 1972 by Frederick Ungar Publishing Co., Inc. Reprinted by permission.

52. S. S. Prawer, *German Lyric Poetry, A Critical Analysis of Selected Poems from Klopstock to Rilke* (London: Routledge & Kegan Paul, 1952), p. 175.

53. Ibid., p. 176.

54. Ibid.

55. *Der Briefwechsel zwischen Theodor Storm und Gottfried Keller*, p. 91.

56. Ibid., p. 112.

57. Ibid.

58. Friedrich Bruns, *Die Lese der deutschen Lyrik von Klopstock bis Rilke* (New York: Appleton-Century-Crofts, 1961), p. 44.

59. Heinrich Henel, *The Poetry of Conrad Ferdinand Meyer* (Madison: University of Wisconsin Press, 1954), pp. viii, 56.

60. Werner Oberle, "Conrad Ferdinand Meyer, Ein Forschungsbericht," *Germanisch-Romanische Monatsschrift* 37 (1956): 243.

61. Henel, *The Poetry of Conrad Ferdinand Meyer*, p. 7.

62. Ibid., p. 41.

63. In vol. 53 (1884): 266–71.

64. *Fontanes Briefe in zwei Bänden*, ed. G. Erler, II (Berlin and Weimar: Aufbau, 1968), p. 362.

65. *Gedichte Conrad Ferdinand Meyers, Wege ihrer Vollendung*, ed. H. Henel (Tübingen: Niemeyer, 1962), p. 171.

66. Conrad Ferdinand Meyer, *Gedichte*, 4th enl. ed.—the poet's own last important revised ed. (Leipzig: Haessel, 1891), p. 152.

67. Betsy Meyer, *Conrad Ferdinand Meyer in der Erinnerung seiner Schwester* (Berlin: Paetel, 1903), p. 164.

68. Cf. Paul Böckmann, "Deutsche Lyrik im 19. Jahrhundert," *Formkräfte der deutschen Dichtung vom Barock bis zur Gegenwart*, ed. H. Steffen, 2nd ed. (Göttingen: Vandenhoeck & Ruprecht, 1967), p. 185.

Chapter Four

1. Geoffrey and Kathleen Tillotson, *Mid-Victorian Studies* (London: Athlone, 1965), p. 24.

2. *Westminster Review* 14 (1858): 491.

3. Edmond et Jules de Goncourt, *Journal, Mémoires de la vie littéraire*, ed. R. Ricatte, X (Monaco: Les Éditions de L'Imprimerie Nationale de Monaco, 1956), p. 35.

4. W. D. Howells, "Some Anomalies of the Short Story," *North American Review* 173 (1901): 425–26.

5. *Revue des Deux Mondes*, March 1, 1857, pp. 33–65.

6. *Die Grenzboten*, 1856, IV, 121.

7. Schmidt, *Characterbilder aus der zeitgenössischen Literatur* (Leipzig: Duncker & Humblot, 1875), p. 186.

8. "Otto Ludwigs Stellung zur Revolution von 1848 nach seinen Briefen an Ludwig Ambrunn," *Otto Ludwig Jahrbuch* 11 (1939): 83–84.

9. Ibid., p. 91.

10. Ibid., p. 83.

11. *Otto Ludwigs Gesammelte Schriften*, ed. A. Stern (Leipzig: Grunow, 1891), VI, p. 420.

12. Cf. Alfred Schwarz, "Otto Ludwig's Shakespearean Criticism," *Perspectives of Criticism*, ed. H. Levin (Cambridge, Mass.: Harvard University Press, 1950), p. 100.

13. *Ludwigs Gesammelte Schriften*, V, p. 459.

14. Ibid., V, p. 271.

15. Ibid., V, pp. 264, 458.

16. Heinrich Reinhardt, *Die Dichtungstheorie der sogenannten Poetischen Realisten* (Würzburg: Triltsch, 1939), pp. 37–89.

17. Richard Brinkmann, *Wirklichkeit und Illusion*, 2nd ed. (Tübingen: Niemeyer, 1966), pp. 3–4.

18. René Wellek, *Concepts of Criticism*, 5th printing, (New Haven and London: Yale University Press, 1969), p. 226.

19. Schmidt, *Characterbilder aus der zeitgenössischen Literatur*, p. 186.

20. *Ludwigs Gesammelte Schriften*, VI, p. 18.

21. Ibid., VI, p. 223.

22. *Westminster Review* 14 (1858): 499.

23. *Athenaeum*, November 26, 1910, p. 668.

24. Barker Fairley, *Wilhelm Raabe, An Introduction to His Novels* (Oxford: Clarendon, 1961), p. 182.

25. Wilhelm Raabe, *Sämtliche Werke*, ed. K. Hoppe et al., I (Göttingen: Vandenhoeck & Ruprecht, 1965), p. 11.

26. Ibid., p. 166.

27. *Correspondance de Georg Brandes*, ed. P. Krüger, III (Copenhagen: Rosenkilde og Bagger, 1966), p. 362.

28. *Die Grenzboten*, 1854, I, 405; 1855, III, 166.

29. Keller, *Gesammelte Briefe*, III/1, p. 407.

30. *Fontanes Briefe in zwei Bänden*, II, p. 363.

31. Mann, *The Genesis of a Novel*, trans. Richard and Clara Winston (London: Secker & Warburg, 1961), p. 147.

32. Keller, *Gesammelte Briefe*, IV, p. 255.

33. Keller, *Sämtliche Werke*, III, ed. J. Fränkel (Zurich and Munich: Rentsch, 1926), pp. 1–2. All other quotations from this novel are translations of passages in this edition.

34. Keller, *Gesammelte Briefe*, III/1, p. 347.

35. Petersen's correspondence with Keller, as yet only partially published, is deposited in the Zentralbibliothek at Zurich. The Bayerische Staatsbibliothek in Munich and the Schleswig-Holsteinische Landesbibliothek in Kiel own large collections of his unpublished letters to other writers. The quotations in our account are taken, unless otherwise indicated, from unpublished letters. Other source information is from an unpublished manuscript by Lorenz Petersen, *Wilhelm Petersen, Zu seinem hundertjährigen Geburtstage am 20. Januar 1935*, now in the Schleswig-Holsteinische Landesbibliothek.

36. Keller, *Gesammelte Briefe*, III/1, p. 354.

Chapter Five

1. Storm, *Sämtliche Werke*, ed. A. Köster, VIII, p. 97.

2. Fontane, *Sämtliche Werke*, XX, p. 40.

3. C. Fillingham Coxwell, *German Poetry translated into English in the Original Metres* (London: Daniel, 1938), p. 180. The exigencies of copyright have prevented us from changing the last word of the second line from *slightly* to *tightly*, which, we think, would have been preferable.

4. For the fullest discussion of this subject see Walter Müller-Seidel, *Theodor Fontane, Soziale Romankunst in Deutschland* (Stuttgart: Metzler, 1975).

5. *Meyer-Rodenberg Briefwechsel*, p. 296.

6. Schmidt, *Bilder aus dem geistigen Leben unserer Zeit*, I (Leipzig: Duncker & Humblot, 1871), p. 411.

7. Mann, *Gesammelte Werke*, X, 358–60. Cf. also Brian A. Rowley, "Theodor Fontane: A German Novelist in the European Tradition?," *German Life & Letters*, 15 (1961): 83.

8. Fontane, *Briefe an die Freunde*, ed. F. Fontane and H. Fricke, II (Berlin: Grote, 1943), p. 585.

9. Peter Demetz, *Formen des Realismus: Theodor Fontane* (Munich: Hanser, 1964), pp. 164–77.

10. For details see the afterword in Sven-Aage Jørgensen's edition of *Unwiederbringlich* (Stuttgart: Reclam, 1971).

11. Oskar Seidlin, *Essays in German and Comparative Literature* (Chapel Hill: University of North Carolina Press, 1961), p. 1.

Chapter Six

1. *Der Briefwechsel zwischen Theodor Fontane und Paul Heyse*, ed. G. Erler (Berlin and Weimar: Aufbau, 1972), p. 205.

2. *Der Briefwechsel von Emanuel Geibel und Paul Heyse*, ed. E. Petzet (Munich: Lehmann, 1922), p. 1.

3. *Die Grenzboten*, 1854, III, 72–73; IV, 403; 1855, I, 386; 1859, IV, 499.

4. Schmidt, *Bilder aus dem geistigen Leben unserer Zeit*, I, pp. 410–27; *Characterbilder aus der zeitgenössischen Literatur*, pp. 340–50.

5. Schmidt, *Bilder aus dem geistigen Leben unserer Zeit*, I, pp. 411, 413, 426.

6. P. H. Traustedt et al., *Dansk Litteratur Historie*, new and enl. ed., III (Copenhagen: Politiken, 1976), p. 23.

7. Kurt Aspelin, *Poesi och verklighet* (Göteborg: Akademiförlaget, 1967), pp. 20–21, 96–106, 110, 280–81, 283.

8. Anders Österling, *Dagens gärning* (Stockholm: Bonnier, 1921), p. 176.

9. Bredsdorff, Mortensen, Popperwell, *An Introduction to Scandinavian Literature* (Copenhagen: Munksgaard, 1951), p. 200; Alrik Gustafson, *A History of Swedish Literature* (Minneapolis: University of Minnesota Press, 1961), pp. 367–68.

Selected Bibliography

1. General Studies

ALKER, ERNST. *Die deutsche Literatur im 19. Jahrhundert 1832–1914,* 3rd ed. Stuttgart: Kröner, 1969. A more wearisome than informative history of German literature during the past century; but if a reader is looking for an almost complete set of names, titles, and dates, this is certainly the book he will want to consult.

AUST, HUGO. *Literatur des Realismus.* Stuttgart: Metzler, 1977. An unassuming but reliable little guide to the criticism of the theory and practice of realism in German literature.

BENNETT, E. K. *A History of the German Novelle,* 2nd ed., revised and continued by H. M. Waidson. Cambridge, England: Cambridge University Press, 1961; rpt. 1974. Has become an indispensable handbook in the English-speaking world for those wishing to learn about the novella of Poetic Realism, but is now badly in need of extensive revision. The book's most important sections, those addressed to Poetic Realism, have remained substantially unchanged since the first edition of 1934.

BÖCKMANN, PAUL. "Deutsche Lyrik im 19. Jahrhundert." In *Formkräfte der deutschen Dichtung vom Barock bis zur Gegenwart,* ed. H. Steffen. Göttingen: Vandenhoeck & Ruprecht, 2nd ed., 1967, pp. 165–86. A seminal essay. The best that has been written on the nineteenth-century German lyric, a subject which has more often been treated with eloquent reverence than judicious inquiry.

BOESCHENSTEIN, HERMANN. *German Literature of the Nineteenth Century.* London: Arnold; New York: St. Martin's Press, 1969. The author provides a concise introduction to the entire body of German literature from 1830 to the end of the century, and adds to his account an uncommon blend of assurance, wisdom, and elegant writing.

BÖTTCHER, KURT, et al. *Geschichte der deutschen Literatur von 1830 bis zum Ausgang des 19. Jahrhunderts,* 2 vols. Berlin: Volk und Wissen, 1975. This is a collective undertaking by a group of Marxist scholars seeking to give a new coherence to the history of German literature from 1830 to the end of the century. The post-1848 age looms heavily as a distinct entity.

BRINKMANN, RICHARD. *Wirklichkeit und Illusion*, 2nd ed. Tübingen: Niemeyer, 1966. Addresses itself to the problem of realism in nineteenth-century German fiction and comes to the conclusion that the more realistic a work is, the more it tends to become subjective. René Wellek has called the argument "idiosyncratic" (*Concepts of Criticism*, p. 237), while other scholars have protested, rightly, that in a book of this sort the theoretical writings of Julian Schmidt are as blithely ignored as the works of Keller, Storm, Meyer, Raabe, and Fontane. Yet, after all has been said, the volume remains the product of a sensitive critic whose subtle analyses help to further the study of Poetic Realism.

————, ed. *Begriffsbestimmung des literarischen Realismus*, 2nd ed. Darmstadt: Wissenschaftliche Buchgesellschaft, 1974. A motley group of essays by various hands on the literary problem of realism in the nineteenth century. Opinions conflict and clash, but the volume's overriding picture is certainly exciting.

BUCHER, MAX, et al. *Realismus und Gründerzeit, Manifeste und Dokumente zur deutschen Literatur 1848–1880*, 2 vols. Stuttgart: Metzler, 1975 & 1976. A gold mine of background material for the study of Poetic Realism.

COWEN, ROY C. *Neunzehntes Jahrhundert (1830–1880)*. Berne and Munich: Francke, 1970. A most useful bibliographical tool.

DAVID, CLAUDE. *Zwischen Romantik und Symbolismus 1820–1885*. Gütersloh: Mohn, 1966. Offers refreshing reading, for it passes judgment freely and easily. Interesting, too, because it draws upon the author's knowledge of French realism for its critical assessments.

EISELE, ULF. *Realismus und Ideologie, Zur Kritik der literarischen Theorie nach 1848 am Beispiel des "Deutschen Museums."* Stuttgart: Metzler, 1976. In his carefully written and well-documented book, the author builds up a picture of the theory of realism as it emerged from the pages of an important literary journal in the years 1851–1867. The reader observes how the argument of Julian Schmidt is continued, varied, and refined.

————. "Realismus-Problematik: Überlegungen zur Forschungssituation," *Deutsche Vierteljahrsschrift für Literaturwissenschaft und Geistesgeschichte* 51 (1977): 148–74. A thoughtful discussion of recent studies concerned with the theory of realism in mid-nineteenth-century Germany.

ERMATINGER, EMIL. *Deutsche Dichter 1750–1900, Eine Geistesgeschichte in Lebensbildern*, 2nd ed., revised by J. Göres. Frankfurt/M. and Bonn: Athenäum, 1961. A standard work of German literary scholarship in new attractive dress. The Poetic Realists are given extensive biographical coverage.

FEHR, KARL. "Realism (1830–1885)." In *German Literature, A Critical Sur-*

vey, ed. B. Boesch, trans. R. Taylor. London: Methuen, 1971, pp. 254–89. This essay, lucidly translated from the German, offers a lively introduction to the years 1830–1885 in German literature, but it does not escape the danger of superficiality.

FUERST, NORBERT. *The Victorian Age of German Literature, Eight Essays.* University Park and London: The Pennsylvania State University Press, 1966. A perceptive presentation of the warp and woof of German literature from 1820 to 1880. Regrettably, however, Groth, Ludwig, Raabe, and Storm are not discussed.

HERMAND, JOST. "Zur Literatur der Gründerzeit," *Deutsche Vierteljahrsschrift für Literaturwissenschaft und Geistesgeschichte* 41 (1967): 202–32. Reprinted in J. Hermand, *Von Mainz nach Weimar (1793–1919).* Stuttgart: Metzler, 1969, pp. 211–49. A crisp and impassioned inquiry into the question of when the post-1848 movement in German literature properly ended. Highly provocative. The only study of its kind, it should be read by everyone interested in the age.

JÄGER, HANS-WOLF. "Gesellschaftliche Aspekte des bürgerlichen Realismus und seiner Theorie, Bemerkungen zu Julian Schmidt und Gustav Freytag," *Text & Kontext* 2:3 (1974): 3–41. A stimulating lecture delivered at a Danish university. Particularly useful because of the attention it draws to Schmidt.

KAHRMANN, BERND, et al. "Bürgerlicher Realismus," *Wirkendes Wort* 23 (1973): 53–68; 24 (1974): 339–56; 26 (1976): 356–81. Surveys some of the scholarship of the years 1968–1973 addressed to German literature in the second half of the nineteenth century.

KINDER, HERMANN. *Poesie als Synthese, Ausbreitung eines deutschen Realismus-Verständnisses in der Mitte des 19. Jahrhunderts.* Frankfurt/M.: Athenäum, 1973. Remarkably good introduction to the theory of realism in German nineteenth-century literature. Should be read in conjunction with the books by H. Widhammer (see below).

KOHLSCHMIDT, WERNER. *Geschichte der deutschen Literatur vom Jungen Deutschland bis zum Naturalismus.* Stuttgart: Reclam, 1975. Deals at considerable length with the leading writers of German Poetic Realism. The author manages to convey, without ever being tedious, much of the flavor of the movement. Yet the book has annoying flaws: for a modern work of its magnitude (919 pp.), there is no excuse for dismissing the enormous impact of the 1848 revolutions on the literature of the time, nor is it excusable to avoid discussing the seminal role played by Julian Schmidt. Equally detrimental to the book is the effect of splitting the major authors into different camps (Otto Ludwig is linked with Droste-Hülshoff in one section, Fontane with the pre-1848 writer Jeremias Gotthelf in another). This leaves us with nothing but a loose conception of Poetic Realism, deprived of all objective qualities.

LÖWITH, KARL. *From Hegel to Nietzsche, The Revolution in Nineteenth-*

Century Thought, trans. D. E. Green. New York: Holt, Rinehart and Winston, 1964; rpt. Garden City, N.Y.: Doubleday, 1967. An exciting guide through the maze of German intellectual history in the middle of the nineteenth century. Excellent background material for the study of Poetic Realism. The German original of this book had attracted a wide circle of readers in the 1950s and 1960s, not least of all because of a brilliant clarity of expression, which is lost in the dreary (although adequate) English translation.

LUKÁCS, GEORG. *Skizze einer Geschichte der neueren deutschen Literatur.* Neuwied: Luchterhand, 1963; rpt. 1975. In the central chapter of this little book, an uncommonly alert mind stubbornly and rightly insists that German literature in the second half of the nineteenth century cannot be separated from the context of the 1848 revolutions. Has been translated into French, Hungarian, Italian, and Japanese but, alas, not into English.

MARKWARDT, BRUNO. *Geschichte der deutschen Poetik. Band IV: Das neunzehnte Jahrhundert.* Berlin: de Gruyter, 1959. A bulky, encyclopedic book which, if looked at for more than five minutes, tends to pall and depress. René Wellek has correctly remarked that the author had "studied the most casual pronouncements of fifth-rate writers, classifying their theories into the strangest pigeonholes" (*Concepts of Criticism,* p. 235). Patient and discriminating readers, however, can profit from the extensive discussions of Poetic Realism.

MARTINI, FRITZ. *Deutsche Literatur im bürgerlichen Realismus, 1848–1898,* 3rd ed. Stuttgart: Metzler, 1974. Unquestionably the fullest available account of the post-1848 period in German literature. The book is vast in scope and rich in detail, solid and brilliant, stimulating and illuminating. Its author clearly has a sovereign command of the subject. The reader, however, easily gets lost in the microcosms of the age.

———. *Forschungsbericht zur deutschen Literatur in der Zeit des Realismus.* Stuttgart: Metzler, 1962. Offers a fascinating survey of modern scholarship addressed to German literature in the second half of the nineteenth century. Distinguished by the great critical acumen of its author.

PREISENDANZ, WOLFGANG. *Humor als dichterische Einbildungskraft, Studien zur Erzählkunst des poetischen Realismus,* 2nd ed. Munich: Fink, 1976. The most thought-provoking book that has ever addressed itself to the aesthetic problem of Poetic Realism. It deserves to be widely read and studied.

———. *Wege des Realismus, Zur Poetik und Erzählkunst im 19. Jahrhundert.* Munich: Fink, 1977. A collection of brilliant essays continuing the argument of the above-mentioned book. The fourth essay, "Voraussetzungen des poetischen Realismus in der deutschen Erzählkunst des 19. Jahrhunderts," makes for particularly rewarding reading.

RITCHIE, J. M. "The Ambivalence of 'Realism' in German Literature 1830–1880," *Orbis Litterarum* 15 (1960): 200–17 (German translation in *Begriffsbestimmung des literarischen Realismus,* ed. R. Brinkmann, 2nd ed. Darmstadt: Wissenschaftliche Buchgesellschaft, 1974, pp. 376–99).

———. "Realism." In *Periods in German Literature,* ed. J. M. Ritchie. London: Oswald Wolff, 1966, pp. 171–95.

———. "Realism in Germany, from the Death of Goethe." In *The Age of Realism,* ed. F. W. J. Hemmings. Harmondsworth, England and Baltimore: Penguin Books, 1974, pp. 218–64. Three companion essays which sustain and spark interest at every turn. They have been written by a well-known English authority on Poetic Realism and carry great conviction.

SAGARRA, EDA. *Tradition and Revolution, German Literature and Society 1830–1890.* London: Weidenfeld and Nicolson, 1971. A lively and eminently readable book which traces the course of nineteenth-century German literature against the multicolored backdrop of contemporary social change and cultural debate. Available in German translation. Munich: List, 1972.

SILZ, WALTER. *Realism and Reality, Studies in the German Novelle of Poetic Realism,* 4th printing. Chapel Hill: University of North Carolina Press, 1965. This volume has become a classic in its own time.

STAHL, E. L., and YUILL, W. E. *German Literature of the Eighteenth and Nineteenth Centuries.* London: Cresset Press, 1970. The final section of this book contains a brief panoramic survey of the second half of the nineteenth century; it is delightfully free of the tedium which frequently attends historical description.

STERN, J. P. *Idylls and Reality, Studies in Nineteenth-Century German Literature.* London: Methuen; New York: Ungar, 1971.

———. "German Literature in the Age of European Realism." In *German Language and Literature: Seven Essays,* ed. K. Weimar. Englewood Cliffs, N.J.: Prentice-Hall, 1974, pp. 223–306. The Poetic Realists receive, alas, only secondary attention in these two uncommonly eloquent and entertaining studies.

WIDHAMMER, HELMUTH. *Realismus und klassizistische Tradition, Zur Theorie der Literatur in Deutschland 1848–1860.* Tübingen: Niemeyer, 1972.

———. *Die Literaturtheorie des deutschen Realismus 1848–1860.* Stuttgart: Metzler, 1977. Two books that have much in common with the one by H. Kinder (see above), and yet are strikingly different.

WIESE, BENNO VON, ed. *Deutsche Dichter des 19. Jahrhunderts, Ihr Leben und Werk,* 2nd ed. Berlin: Erich Schmidt, 1979. A collection of essays by diverse scholars, mostly of high standard and covering individual Poetic Realists.

WINTERSCHEIDT, FRIEDRICH. *Deutsche Unterhaltungsliteratur der Jahre 1850–1860.* Bonn: Bouvier, 1970. The reader of this book will learn much about the important minor writers in Germany when Poetic Realism was on the rise.

2. Studies on Individual Works

a. Keller's "Abendlied"

PRAWER, S. S. *German Lyric Poetry, A Critical Analysis of Selected Poems from Klopstock to Rilke.* London: Routledge & Kegan Paul, 1952; rpt. New York: Barnes & Noble, 1965. Keller's most accomplished poem is brilliantly analyzed in this volume.

b. Storm's *Aquis submersus*

BERND, CLIFFORD A. *Theodor Storm's Craft of Fiction,* 2nd ed. Chapel Hill: University of North Carolina Press, 1966. In this book the reader will find the most detailed modern analysis of *Aquis submersus.*

BOSWELL, PATRICIA M., ed. *Theodor Storm, Aquis submersus.* Oxford: Basil Blackwell, 1974. The long introduction to this volume (over fifty pages) offers an extraordinarily engaging commentary on the novella. Quite invaluable.

c. Raabe's *Die Chronik der Sperlingsgasse*

DIETZE, WALTER. "Zeitstimmung und Zeitkritik in Wilhelm Raabes 'Chronik der Sperlingsgasse,'" *Monatshefte* 61 (1969): 337–41. This certainly is an enthusiastic article, bringing up a plethora of exciting ideas. With a gimlet mind the author takes issue with those critics who would regard this novel as anything less than a veritable masterpiece of fiction.

FAIRLEY, BARKER. *Wilhelm Raabe, An Introduction to His Novels.* Oxford: Clarendon, 1961. Everyone will find himself richly rewarded after he has read the chapter on *Die Chronik der Sperlingsgasse* in this outstanding book. Available in German translation. Munich: Beck, 1961.

d. Keller's *Der grüne Heinrich*

PASCAL, ROY. *The German Novel.* Manchester and Toronto: The University Press, 1956; rpt. 1965. Critics will want to read the extremely lucidly written study of *Der grüne Heinrich* included in this volume. It abounds with flashes of great insight.

PREISENDANZ, WOLFGANG. "Keller, Der grüne Heinrich." In *Der deutsche Roman vom Barock bis zur Gegenwart,* ed. B. von Wiese. Düsseldorf: Bagel, 2nd ed. 1973, II, 76–127. Reprinted in W. Preisendanz, *Wege des Realismus.* Munich: Fink, 1977, pp. 127–80. An authoritative treatment by a brilliant scholar.

ROMBERG, BERTIL. *Studies in the Narrative Technique of the First-Person Novel.* Stockholm: Almqvist & Wiksell, 1962; rpt. Folcroft, Pa.: Folcroft Library Editions, 1973. An eminent Swedish critic includes, in this weighty tome, an absorbing discussion of the narrative structure of *Der grüne Heinrich.*

SWALES, MARTIN. *The German Bildungsroman from Wieland to Hesse.* Princeton: Princeton University Press, 1978. Offers a fresh interpretation of *Der grüne Heinrich* against the backdrop of a peculiarly German tradition of the novel.

e. Meyer's *Der Heilige*

BÖKER, UWE. "C. F. Meyers *Der Heilige,* Die Bedeutung der Erzählhaltung für die Interpretation der Novelle," *Studia Neophilologica* 39 (1967): 60–79. A penetrating study.

COUPE, W. A., ed. *Conrad Ferdinand Meyer, Der Heilige,* 2nd impression. Oxford: Basil Blackwell, 1971. The very comprehensive and admirably concise introduction to this volume offers the most thought-provoking interpretation of the novella that has ever been written. Highly recommended reading!

HERTLING, GUNTER H. *Conrad Ferdinand Meyers Epik: Traumbeseelung, Traumbesinnung und Traumbesitz.* Berne: Francke, 1973. Deserves mention because it has an important chapter on *Der Heilige.* But the book must be used with caution, for Mary C. Crichton has pointed out that it contains "numerous slightly loose and some plainly wrong uses of quotations, and other flaws." (*Journal of English and Germanic Philology* 74 [1975]: 78).

SILZ, WALTER. "Meyer, *Der Heilige.*" In *Realism and Reality, Studies in the German Novelle of Poetic Realism,* 4th printing. Chapel Hill: University of North Carolina Press, 1965, pp. 94–116. The classic interpretation of this novella.

WILLIAMS, W. D. *The Stories of C. F. Meyer.* Oxford: Clarendon, 1962. *Der Heilige* receives considerable attention in this book, but the account is little more than a laborious discussion of plot and character.

f. Storm's *Immensee*

McHAFFIE, M. A., and RITCHIE, J. M. "Bee's Lake, or the Curse of Silence, A Study of Theodor Storm's *Immensee,*" *German Life & Letters* 16 (1962): 36–48. Owing to its critical analysis of the novella, scene by scene, and because of its stimulating comparison of Storm's work with Mann's *Tonio Kröger,* this essay is extremely valuable.

SAMMERN-FRANKENEGG, FRITZ RÜDIGER. *Perspektivische Strukturen einer*

Erinnerungsdichtung, Studien zur Deutung von Storms "Immensee." Stuttgart: Hans-Dieter Heinz, 1976. By far the most extensive and informative study of this incomparably popular novella.

g. Storm's "Meeresstrand"

MERKER, PAUL. "Theodor Storm: Meeresstrand." In *Gedicht und Gedanke,* ed. H. O. Burger. Halle: Niemeyer, 1942, pp. 274–87. A fascinating piece of criticism. To read it is like seeing the poet conduct a magnificent orchestra.

h. Meyer's "Der römische Brunnen"

HART, THOMAS ELWOOD. "Linguistic Patterns, Literary Structure, and the Genesis of C. F. Meyer's 'Der römische Brunnen,' " *Language and Style* 4 (1971): 83–115. A very substantial examination. Argues for a return to Meyer's own authorized orthography when reading the poem, a practice not common today.

RYDER, FRANK G. " 'Der römische Brunnen'—Sound Pattern and Content," *Monatshefte* 52 (1960): 235–41. The interpretation of the poem took an unusually firm step forward with this well-documented analysis of some of its most significant linguistic features.

i. Keller's *Romeo und Julia auf dem Dorfe*

KAISER, GERHARD. "Sündenfall, Paradies und himmlisches Jerusalem in Kellers 'Romeo und Julia auf dem Dorfe,' " *Euphorion* 65 (1971): 21–48. Reprinted in G. Kaiser, *Wandrer und Idylle*. Göttingen: Vandenhoeck & Ruprecht, 1977, pp. 258–89. The author, in a most telling fashion, argues a stimulating thesis.

MCCORMICK, E. ALLEN. "The Idylls in Keller's *Romeo und Julia*: A Study in Ambivalence," *German Quarterly* 35 (1962): 265–79. Slapdash in its treatment of the theme of ambivalence, as G. Kaiser (see above) has noted; but otherwise a rewarding exploration of the idyllic scenes in this novella.

REHDER, HELMUT. "Romeo und Julia auf dem Dorfe, An Analysis," *Monatshefte* 35 (1943): 416–34. Still a very useful close reading of the text.

SILZ, WALTER. "Keller, *Romeo und Julia auf dem Dorfe*." In *Realism and Reality, Studies in the German Novelle of Poetic Realism*, 4th printing. Chapel Hill: University of North Carolina Press, 1965, pp. 79–93. The classic interpretation of this novella.

j. Ludwig's *Zwischen Himmel und Erde*

DICKSON, KEITH A. " 'Die Moral von der Geschicht': Art and Artifice in 'Zwischen Himmel und Erde,' " *Modern Language Review* 68 (1973):

115–28. A learned and entertaining essay by a scholar who is well acquainted with the subject matter.

LILLYMAN, WILLIAM J. *Otto Ludwig's "Zwischen Himmel und Erde," A Study of Its Artistic Structure.* The Hague and Paris: Mouton, 1967. An exemplary book. The most comprehensive and subtle analysis of this novel available. Indispensable for further scholarship.

THOMAS, LIONEL. "Otto Ludwig's *Zwischen Himmel und Erde,*" *Proceedings of the Leeds Philosophical and Literary Society* 16 (1975): Part 2, 27–38. Intuitive and informative. Written by a critic who is extraordinarily widely read in nineteenth-century literature.

Index